# THE SILENT LANGUAGE

Also by Edward T. Hall

BEYOND CULTURE (Anchor Books)

THE HIDDEN DIMENSION (Anchor Books)

THE DANCE OF LIFE:
The Other Dimension of Time (Anchor Books)

HIDDEN DIFFERENCES:
Doing Business with the Japanese
(with Mildred Reed Hall) (Anchor Books)

HANDBOOK FOR PROXEMIC RESEARCH

THE FOURTH DIMENSION IN ARCHITECTURE:
The Impact of Building on Man's Behavior
(with Mildred Reed Hall)

THE SILENT LANGUAGE

EDWARD T. HALL

ANCHOR BOOKS
A DIVISION OF RANDOM HOUSE, INC.
NEW YORK

TO

my friends and colleagues from foreign cultures who taught me so much about my own culture.

ANCHOR BOOKS EDITIONS: 1973,1990

Copyright © 1959, 1981 by Edward T. Hall

Library of Congress Cataloging-in-Publication Data
Hall, Edward Twitchell, 1914–
   The silent language / Edward T. Hall.
    p. cm.
   Includes bibliographical references.
   1. Intercultural communication. I. Title.
HM258.H245 1990   90-164
303.48'2—dc20   CIP
ISBN 0-385-05549-8

www.anchorbooks.com

Printed in the United States of America
38 37 36 35 34 33

CONTENTS

v

INTRODUCTION

Over thirty years have elapsed since *The Silent Language* first appeared. In this interval, many things happened to validate the basic tenets of this book. However, when it was published I was so closely involved in my own work that I failed to fully appreciate the magnitude of the need for cross-cultural insights and observations.

Actually, *The Silent Language* is a translation not from one language to another, but from a series of complex, nonverbal, contexting communications into words. The title summarizes not only the content of the book, but one of the great paradoxes of culture. It isn't just that people "talk" to each other without the use of words, but that there is an entire universe of behavior that is unexplored, unexamined, and very much taken for granted. It functions outside conscious awareness and *in juxtaposition to words*. Those of us of European heritage live in a "word world" which we think is real, but just because we talk doesn't mean the rest of what we communicate with our behavior is not equally important. While there can be no doubt that language molds thinking in particularly subtle ways, mankind must eventually come to grips with the reality of other cultural systems and the pervasive effect these other systems exert on how the world is perceived, *how the self is experienced*, and how life itself is organized. We must also accustom ourselves to the fact that messages on the word level can mean one thing and that sometimes something quite different is being communicated on another level. Thirty years is not enough time to make these points; certainly much more time is needed before all their implications are realized.

The link between language and gestures is much closer than between language and the other cultural systems herein described—time and space, for example. A gesture and a word may be interchangeable, but this is not true for time or space. Space, which is the subject of two books, *The Hidden Dimension* and *The Dance of Life*, not only communicates in the most basic sense, but it also *organizes* virtually everything in life. It is easier to see how space can organize activities and institutions than to recognize the subtle manner in which language arranges the furniture of the mind. What is most difficult to accept is the fact that our own cultural patterns are literally unique, and therefore they are *not* universal. It is this difficulty that human beings have in getting outside their own cultural skins that motivated me to commit my observations and conceptual models to writing.

One of the advantages of having written a book which survives the temporary whims of fashion is that one gets feedback from readers—not only words of encouragement, but validation with examples. I wish to express my deep appreciation to those who have written to me from all over the world. The book has been translated into Chinese, Dutch, Polish, French, Italian, and Serbo-Croatian.

For many years I was involved with the selection and

training of Americans working in foreign countries for both government and business. I remain convinced that much of our difficulty with people in other countries stems from the fact that so little is known about cross-cultural communication. Because of this, most of the good will and great efforts of our nation have been wasted in our foreign aid programs. When Americans are sent abroad to deal with foreigners, they should first be carefully selected for their suitability. Then for their own comfort and to insure their effectiveness, they should be taught to speak and read the language of the country, and thoroughly informed about the culture. All of this takes time and costs money. However, unless we are willing to select and train personnel, we simply waste our time and money overseas.

Formal training in language, history, government, and customs is only a first step. Of equal importance is an introduction to the nonverbal language of the country. Most Americans are only dimly aware of this "silent language" even though they use it every day. They are not conscious of the elaborate patterning of behavior which prescribes the handling of time, spatial relationships, attitudes towards work, play, and learning. In addition to our verbal language, we are constantly communicating our real feelings in the language of behavior.

Difficulties in intercultural communication are seldom seen for what they are. When it becomes apparent to people of different countries that they are not understanding one another, each tends to blame "those foreigners," for their stupidity, deceit, or craziness as the following example illustrates.

Despite a host of favorable auspices, an American aid mission in Greece was having great difficulty working out an agreement. Efforts to negotiate met with resistance and suspicion on the part of the Greeks, and consequently the Americans were unable to conclude the agreements. A later analysis of this exasperating situation revealed two unsuspected reasons for the stalemate: First, Americans pride themselves on being outspoken and forthright, while these same qualities are regarded as a liability by the Greeks. Forthrightness indicates a lack of finesse which the Greeks deplore. Second, the unspoken rule for meetings in the United States is to limit the length of the meeting according to schedule and to reach agreements on general principles first, delegating the drafting of details to subordinates. The Greeks regarded this practice as a device to pull the wool over their eyes. Greek custom calls for working out details in front of all concerned, which necessitates continuing meetings for as long as necessary and not being bound by a schedule. The result of this misunderstanding was a series of unproductive meetings with each side deploring the other's behavior. American behavior said to the Greeks: "Not only do these fellows act like peasants lacking finesse, but by devious scheduling and tricks, they try to pull the wool over our eyes."

It is essential that we understand how other people read our behavior (not our words, but our behavior). If this book does nothing more than plant this idea, it will have served its purpose. However, I have a more ambitious goal. This book was written for those who are committed to the improvement of the human situation and who want to learn more about the *cultural unconscious*. Those persons who are at times perplexed by life, who feel driven by forces they do not understand, who may see others doing things that genuinely mystify them at home and overseas should find some solace in these pages. I hope to show the reader that behind the apparent mystery, confusion, and disorganization of life there *is* order. This understanding will perhaps lead him/her to re-examine human behavior in the world around him. I hope too that it will also interest readers in the subject of culture and lead them to follow their own intuition and make their own observations.

In my research on culture, I initially received invaluable collaboration from my colleague, George L. Trager. Trager is an anthropologically trained linguist who has made important contributions to the study of language. Trager and I developed a theory of culture based on a communications model which is contained in this book and which provides its theoretical underpinning.

The pages that follow have been arranged to lead the reader gradually from the known to the unknown. It will be helpful if the reader thinks of culture as analogous to music: a) If another person hasn't heard a particular piece of music, it is impossible to describe. b) Before the days of written scores, people had to learn informally by imitation. c) People were able to exploit the potential of music only when they started writing musical scores. This is what must be done for culture, and this book represents the cultural analogue of a musical primer.

The non-American reader as well as members of many American subcultures should remember that this book was written primarily as a message to the author's own group in an effort to increase their understanding of their own unconscious culture. Because outsiders make poor spokesmen and seldom really master another culture, one would hope that similar volumes will eventually be written by the Spanish groups, the Native Americans, and the ethnic blacks. I hope the study of unconscious culture (micro-culture) will be carried on and encouraged elsewhere in the world, because the future of the human race lies in maintaining its diversity and turning that diversity to its advantage.

My first acknowledgment, as always, goes to a person whom I have learned to appreciate, love, and admire as we have collaborated over the years—my wife and part-

ner, Mildred Reed Hall. Her contribution to anything I
have done has always been substantial.

As an anthropologist and a scientist I owe a tremendous
debt to my colleagues, but especially to the late Ralph
Linton, under whom I studied at Columbia University.
We spent many pleasant hours together as he tried out
ideas he was developing in an amazing range of subjects.
As a student I found it difficult to communicate with
professors, but with Linton the gulf experienced with
other professors was never present. He always seemed
able to communicate clearly and enjoy a real exchange of
ideas. While the content of this book is different from
anything Linton would have written, I feel that he would
have understood at least some of the ideas. In the world
of ideas he was innovative and particularly free from the
constraints that bind many intellectuals, and his contributions to anthropology were considerable.

Three other colleagues who provided encouragement
and stimulation over the years are the late Erich Fromm,
David Riesman, and John Useem. Although I never knew
her well, Ruth Benedict also provided an intellectual role
model in her excellent innovative books *Patterns of Culture*
and *The Chrysanthemum and the Sword*.

Many of my observations on other cultures are the
direct result of fieldwork with the Spanish-Americans in
New Mexico and Latin America, the Navajo, Hopi,
Trukese, Western Mediterranean Arabs, and Iranians.
Needless to say, the anthropologist always owes a great
debt to the people he or she works with, because it is
what the anthropologist learns about their cultures that
makes his or her own culture more meaningful.

Clarkson N. Potter first urged me to write this book
and provided the necessary encouragement and understanding for its completion. I wish to express my appreciation for significant editorial assistance to Richard K.
Winslow and Kermit Lansner.

1

THE VOICES
OF TIME

Time talks. It speaks more plainly than words. The message it conveys comes through loud and clear. Because it is manipulated less consciously, it is subject to less distortion than the spoken language. It can shout the truth where words lie.

I was once a member of a mayor's committee on human relations in a large city. My assignment was to estimate what the chances were of non-discriminatory practices being adopted by the different city departments. The first step in this project was to interview the department heads, two of whom were themselves members of minority groups. If one were to believe the words of these officials, it seemed that all of them were more than willing to adopt non-discriminatory labor practices. Yet I felt that, despite what they said, in only one case was there much chance for a change. Why? The answer lay in how they used the silent language of time and space.

Special attention had been given to arranging each interview. Department heads were asked to be prepared to spend an hour or more discussing their thoughts with

1

me. Nevertheless, appointments were forgotten, long waits in outer offices (fifteen to forty-five minutes) were common, and the length of the interview was often cut down to ten or fifteen minutes. I was usually kept at an impersonal distance during the interview. In only one case did the department head come from behind his desk. These men had a position and they were literally and figuratively sticking to it!

The implication of this experience (one which public-opinion pollsters might well heed) is quite obvious. What people do is frequently more important than what they say. In this case the way these municipal potentates handled time was eloquent testimony to what they inwardly believed, for the structure and meaning of time systems, as well as the time intervals, are easy to identify. In regard to being late there are: "mumble something" periods, slight apology periods, mildly insulting periods requiring full apology, rude periods, and downright insulting periods. The psychoanalyst has long been aware of the significance of communication on this level, and can point to the way patients handle time as evidence of "resistances" and "transference."

Different parts of the day, for example, are highly significant in certain contexts. Time may indicate the importance of the occasion as well as on what level an interaction between persons is to take place. In the United States if you telephone someone early in the morning, while he is shaving or she is having breakfast, the time of the call usually signals a matter of utmost importance and extreme urgency. The same applies for calls after 11:00 P.M. A call received during sleeping hours is apt to be taken as a matter of life and death, hence the rude joke value of these calls among the young. Our realization that time talks is even reflected in such common expressions as, "What time does the clock *say?*"

An example of how thoroughly these things are taken

for granted was reported to me by John Useem, an American social anthropologist, in an illuminating case from the South Pacific. The natives of one of the islands had been having a difficult time getting their white supervisors to hire them in a way consistent with their traditional status system. Through ignorance the supervisors had hired too many of one group and by so doing had disrupted the existing balance of power among the natives. The entire population of the island was seething because of this error. Since the Americans continued in their ignorance and refused to hire according to local practice, the head men of the two factions met one night to discuss an acceptable reallocation of jobs. When they finally arrived at a solution, they went en masse to see the plant manager and woke him up to tell him what had been decided. Unfortunately it was then between two and three o'clock in the morning. They did not know that it is a sign of extreme urgency to wake up Americans at this hour. As one might expect, the American plant manager, who understood neither the local language nor the culture nor what the hullabaloo was about, thought he had a riot on his hands and called out the Marines. It simply never occurred to him that the parts of the day have a different meaning for these people than they have for us.

On the other hand, plant managers in the United States are fully aware of the significance of a communication made during the middle of the morning or afternoon that takes everyone away from his work. Whenever they want to make an important announcement they will ask: "When shall we let them know?" In the social world a girl feels insulted when she is asked for a date at the last minute by someone whom she doesn't know very well, and the person who extends an invitation to a dinner party with only three or four days' notice has to apologize. How different from the people of the Middle

East with whom it is pointless to make an appointment too far in advance, because the informal structure of their time system places everything beyond a week into a single category of "future," in which plans tend to "slip off their minds."

Advance notice is often referred to in America as "lead time," an expression which is significant in a culture where schedules are important. While it is learned informally, most of us are familiar with how it works in our own culture, even though we cannot state the rules technically. The rules for lead time in other cultures, however, have rarely been analyzed. At the most they are known by experience to those who lived abroad for some time. Yet think how important it is to know how much time is required to prepare people, or for them to prepare themselves, for things to come. Sometimes lead time would seem to be very extended. At other times, in the Middle East, any period longer than a week may be too long.

How troublesome differing ways of handling time can be is well illustrated by the case of an American agriculturalist assigned to duty as an attaché of our embassy in a Latin country. After what seemed to him a suitable period he let it be known that he would like to call on the minister who was his counterpart. For various reasons, the suggested time was not suitable; all sorts of cues came back to the effect that the time was not yet ripe to visit the minister. Our friend, however, persisted and forced an appointment which was reluctantly granted. Arriving a little before the hour (the American respect pattern), he waited. The hour came and passed; five minutes—ten minutes—fifteen minutes. At this point he suggested to the secretary that perhaps the minister did not know he was waiting in the outer office. This gave him the feeling he had done something concrete and also helped to overcome the great anxiety that was stirring inside him. Twenty minutes—twenty-five minutes—thirty minutes—forty-five minutes (the insult period)!

He jumped up and told the secretary that he had been "cooling his heels" in an outer office for forty-five minutes and he was "damned sick and tired" of this type of treatment. This message was relayed to the minister, who said, in effect, "Let him cool his heels." The attaché's stay in the country was not a happy one.

The principal source of misunderstanding lay in the fact that in the country in question the five-minute-delay interval was not significant. Forty-five minutes, on the other hand, instead of being at the tail end of the waiting scale, was just barely at the beginning. To suggest to an American's secretary that perhaps her boss didn't know you were there after waiting sixty seconds would seem absurd, as would raising a storm about "cooling your heels" for five minutes. Yet this is precisely the way the minister registered the protestations of the American in his outer office! He felt, as usual, that Americans were being totally unreasonable.

Throughout this unfortunate episode the attaché was acting according to the way he had been brought up. At home in the United States his responses would have been normal ones and his behavior legitimate. Yet even if he had been told before he left home that this sort of thing would happen, he would have had difficulty not *feeling* insulted after he had been kept waiting forty-five minutes. If, on the other hand, he had been taught the details of the local time system just as he should have been taught the local spoken language, it would have been possible for him to adjust himself accordingly.

What bothers people in situations of this sort is that they don't realize they are being subjected to another form of communication, one that works part of the time with language and part of the time independently of it.

The fact that the message conveyed is couched in no formal vocabulary makes things doubly difficult, because neither party can get very explicit about what is actually taking place. They can only say what they think is happening and how they feel about it. The thought of what is being communicated is what hurts.

AMERICAN TIME

People of the Western world, particularly Americans, tend to think of time as something fixed in nature, something around us and from which we cannot escape; an ever-present part of the environment, just like the air we breathe. That it might be experienced in any other way seems unnatural and strange, a feeling which is rarely modified even when we begin to discover how really differently it is handled by some other people. Within the West itself certain cultures rank time much lower in over-all importance than we do. In Latin America, for example, time is treated rather cavalierly. In Mexico one commonly hears the expression, "Our time or your time?" *"Hora americana, hora mejicana?"*

As a rule, Americans think of time as a road or a ribbon stretching into the future, along which one progresses. The road has segments or compartments which are to be kept discrete ("one thing at a time"). People who cannot schedule time are looked down upon as impractical. In at least some parts of Latin America, North Americans (their term for us) find themselves annoyed when they have made an appointment with somebody, only to find a lot of other things going on at the same time. An old friend of mine of Spanish cultural heritage used to run his business according to the "Latino" system. This meant that up to fifteen people were in his office at one time. Business which might have been finished in a quarter of an hour sometimes took a whole day. He realized, of course, that the Anglo-Americans were disturbed by this and used to make some allowance for them, a dispensation which meant that they spent only an hour or so in his office when they had planned on a few minutes. The American concept of the discreteness of time and the necessity for scheduling was at variance with this amiable and seemingly confusing Latin system. However, if my friend had adhered to the American system he would have destroyed a vital part of his prosperity. People who came to do business with him also came to find out things and to visit each other. The ten to fifteen Spanish-Americans and Indians who used to sit around the office (among whom I later found myself after I had learned to relax a little) played their own part in a particular type of communications network.

Not only do we Americans segment and schedule time, but we look ahead and are oriented almost entirely toward the future. We like new things and are preoccupied with change. We want to know how to overcome resistance to change. In fact, scientific theories and even some pseudo-scientific ones, which incorporate a striking theory of change, are often given special attention.

Time with us is handled much like a material; we earn it, spend it, save it, waste it. To us it is somewhat immoral to have two things going on at the same time. In Latin America it is not uncommon for one person to have a number of simultaneous jobs which he or she either carries on from one desk or moves between, a small amount of time spent on each.

While we look to the future, our view of it is limited. The future to us is the foreseeable future, not the future of the South Asian that may involve centuries. Indeed, our perspective is so short as to inhibit the operation of a good many practical projects, such as sixty- and one-hundred-year conservation works requiring public support and public funds. Anyone who has worked in industry or in the government of the United States has heard the following: "Gentlemen, this is for the long term! Five or ten years."

For us a "long time" can be almost anything—ten or twenty years, two or three months, a few weeks, or even a couple of days. The South Asian, however, feels that it is perfectly realistic to think of a "long time" in terms of thousands of years or even an endless period. A colleague once described their conceptualization of time as follows: "Time is like a museum with endless corridors and alcoves. You, the viewer, are walking through the museum in the dark, holding a light to each scene as you pass it. God is the curator of the museum, and only He knows all that is in it. One lifetime represents one alcove."

The American's view of the future is linked to a view of the past, for tradition plays an equally limited part in American culture. As a whole, we push it aside or leave it to a few souls who are interested in the past for very special reasons. There are, of course, a few pockets, such as New England and the South, where tradition is emphasized. But in the realm of business, which is the dominant model of United States life, tradition is equated with *experience*, and experience is thought of as being very close to if not synonymous with know-how. Know-how is one of our prized possessions, so that when we look backward it is rarely to take pleasure in the past itself but usually to calculate the know-how, to assess the prognosis for success in the future.

Promptness is also valued highly in American life. If people are not prompt, it is often taken either as an insult or as an indication that they are not quite responsible. There are those, of a psychological bent, who would say that we are obsessed with time. They can point to individuals in American culture who are literally time-ridden. And even the rest of us feel very strongly about time because we have been taught to take it so seriously.

We have stressed this aspect of culture and developed it to a point unequaled anywhere in the world, except, perhaps, in Switzerland and north Germany. Many people criticize our obsessional handling of time. They attribute ulcers and hypertension to the pressure engendered by such a system. Perhaps they are right.

SOME OTHER CONCEPTS OF TIME

Even within the very borders of the United States there are people who handle time in a way which is almost incomprehensible to those who have not made a major effort to understand it. The Pueblo Indians, for example, who live in the Southwest, have a sense of time which is at complete variance with the clock-bound habits of the ordinary American citizen. For the Pueblos events begin when the time is ripe and no sooner.

I can still remember a Christmas dance I attended some twenty-five years ago at one of the pueblos near the Rio Grande. I had to travel over bumpy roads for forty-five miles to get there. At seven thousand feet the ordeal of winter cold at one o'clock in the morning is almost unbearable. Shivering in the still darkness of the pueblo, I kept searching for a clue as to when the dance would begin.

Outside everything was impenetrably quiet. Occasionally there was the muffled beat of a deep pueblo drum, the opening of a door, or the piercing of the night's darkness with a shaft of light. In the church where the dance was to take place a few white townsfolk were huddled together on a balcony, groping for some clue which would suggest how much longer they were going to suffer. "Last year I heard they started at ten o'clock." "They can't start until the priest comes." "There is no way of telling when they will start." All this punctuated by chattering teeth and the stamping of feet to keep up circulation.

Suddenly an Indian opened the door, entered, and poked up the fire in the stove. Everyone nudged his neighbor: "Maybe they are going to begin now." Another hour passed. Another Indian came in from outside, walked across the nave of the church, and disappeared through another door. "Certainly now they will begin. After all, it's almost two o'clock." Someone guessed that they were just being ornery in the hope that the white men would go away. Another had a friend in the pueblo and went to his house to ask when the dance would begin. Nobody knew. Suddenly, when the whites were almost exhausted, there burst upon the night the deep sounds of the drums, rattles, and low male voices singing. Without warning the dance had begun.

After years of performances such as this, no white man in his right mind will hazard a guess as to when one of these ceremonial dances will begin. Those of us who have learned now know that the dance doesn't start at a particular time. It is geared to no schedule. It starts when "things" are ready!

As I pointed out, the white civilized Westerner has a shallow view of the future compared to the Oriental. Yet set beside the Navajo Indians of northern Arizona, he seems a model of long-term patience. The Navajo and the European-American have been trying to adjust their concepts of time for almost a hundred years. So far they have not done too well. To the old-time Navajo time is like space—only the here and now is quite real. The future has little reality to it.

An old friend of mine reared with the Navajo expressed it this way: "You know how the Navajo love horses and how much they love to gamble and bet on horse races. Well, if you were to say to a Navajo, 'My friend, you know my quarter horse that won all the races at Flagstaff last Fourth of July?' that Navajo would eagerly say 'yes, yes,' he knew the horse; and if you were to say, 'In the fall I am going to give you that horse,' the Navajo's face would fall and he would turn around and walk away. On the other hand, if you were to say to him, 'Do you see that old bag of bones I just rode up on? That old hay-bellied mare with the knock-knees and pigeon toes, with the bridle that's falling apart and the saddle that's worn out? You can have that horse, my friend, it's yours. Take it, ride it away now.' Then the Navajo would beam and shake your hand and jump on his new horse and ride away. Of the two, only the immediate gift has reality; a promise of future benefits is not even worth thinking about."

In the early days of the range control and soil conservation programs it was almost impossible to convince the Navajo that there was anything to be gained from giving up their beloved sheep for benefits which could be enjoyed ten or twenty years in the future. Once I was engaged in the supervision of the construction of small earth dams and like everyone else had little success at first in convincing Navajo workmen that they should work hard and build the dam quickly, so that there would be more dams and more water for the sheep. The argument that they could have one dam or ten, depending on how hard they worked, conveyed nothing. It wasn't until I learned to translate our behavior into their terms that they produced as we know they could.

The solution came about in this way. I had been discussing the problem with a friend, Lorenzo Hubbell, who had lived on the reservation all of his life. When there were difficulties I used to find it helpful to unburden myself to him. Somewhere in his remarks there was always a key to the underlying patterns of Navajo life. As we talked I learned that the Navajo understood and respected a bargain. I had some inkling of this when I noticed how unsettled the Indians became when they were permitted to fall down on the job they had agreed to do. In particular they seemed to be apprehensive lest they be asked to repay an unfulfilled obligation at some future time. I decided to sit down with the Navajo crew and talk to them about the work. It was quite useless to argue about the future advantages which would accrue from working hard; linear reasoning and logic were meaningless. They did respond, however, when I indicated that the government was giving them money to get out of debt, providing jobs near their families, and giving them water for their sheep. I stressed the fact that in exchange for this, they must work eight hours every day. This was presented as a bargain. Following my clarification the work progressed satisfactorily.

One of my Indian workmen inadvertently provided another example of the cultural conflict centering around time. His name was "Little Sunday." He was small, wiry, and winning. Since it is not polite to ask the Navajo about their names or even to ask them what their name is, it was necessary to inquire of others how he came to be named "Little Sunday." The explanation was a revealing one.

In the early days of the white traders the Indians had considered difficulty getting used to the fact that we Europeans divided time into strange and unnatural periods instead of having a "natural" succession of days which began with the new moon and ended with the old. They were particularly perplexed by the notion of the week introduced by the traders and the missionaries. Imagine a Navajo Indian living some forty or fifty miles from a trading store that is a hundred miles north of the railroad deciding that he needs flour and maybe a little lard for bread. He thinks about the flour and the lard, and he thinks about his friends and the fun he will have trading, or maybe he wonders if the trader will give him credit or how much money he can get for the hide he has. After riding horseback for a day and a half to two days he reaches the store all ready to trade. The store is locked up tight. There are a couple of other Navajo Indians camped in the hogan built by the trader. They say the trader is inside but he won't trade because it's Sunday. They bang on his door and he tells them, "Go away, it's Sunday," and the Navajo says, "But I came from way up on Black Mesa, and I am hungry. I need some food." What can the trader do? Soon he opens the store and then all the Navajo pour in. One of the most frequent and insistent Sunday visitors was a man who earned for himself the sobriquet "Big Sunday." "Little Sunday," it turns out, ran a close second.

The Sioux Indians provide us with another interesting example of the differing views toward time. Not so long ago a man who was introduced as the superintendent of the Sioux came to my office. I learned that he had been born on the reservation and was a product of both Indian and white cultures, having earned his A.B. at one of the Ivy League colleges.

During a long and fascinating account of the many problems which his tribe was having in adjusting to our way of life, he suddenly remarked: "What would you think of a people who had no word for time? My people have no word for 'late' or for 'waiting,' for that matter. They don't know what it is to wait or to be late." He then continued, "I decided that until they could tell time and knew what time was they could never adjust themselves to white culture. So I set about to teach them time. There wasn't a clock that was running in any of the reservation classrooms. So I first bought some decent clocks. Then I made the school buses start on time, and if an Indian was two minutes late that was just too bad. The bus started at eight forty-two and he had to be there."

He was right, or course. The Sioux could not adjust to European ways until they had learned the meaning of time. The superintendent's methods may have sounded a bit extreme, but they were about the only ones that would work. The idea of starting the buses off and making the drivers hold to a rigid schedule was a stroke of genius, much kinder to the Indian, who could better afford to miss a bus on the reservation than lose a job in town because he was late.

There is, in fact, no other way to teach time to people who handle it as differently from us as the Sioux. The quickest way is to get very technical about it and to make it mean something. Later on these people can learn the informal variations, but until they have experienced and then mastered our type of time they will never adjust to our culture.

Thousands of miles away from the reservations of the American Indian we come to another way of handling time which is apt to be completely unsettling to the unprepared visitor. The inhabitants of the atoll of Truk in the Southwest Pacific treat time in a fashion that has complicated life for themselves as well as for others, since it poses special problems not only for their civil and military governors and the anthropologists recording their life but for their own chiefs as well.

Time does not heal on Truk! Past events stack up, placing an ever-increasing burden on the Trukese and weighing heavily on the present. They are, in fact, treated as though they had just occurred. This was borne out by something which happened shortly after the American occupation of the atoll at the end of World War II.

A villager arrived all out of breath at the military government headquarters. He said that a murder had been committed in the village and that the murderer was running around loose. Quite naturally the military gov-

ernment officer became alarmed. He was about to dis-
patch M.P.s to arrest the culprit when he remembered
that someone had warned him about acting precipitously
when dealing with "natives." A little inquiry turned up
the fact that the victim had been "fooling around" with
the murderer's wife. Still more inquiry of a routine type,
designed to establish the place and date of the crime,
revealed that the murder had not occurred a few hours or
even days ago, as one might have thought, but seventeen
years before. The murderer had been running around
loose in the village all this time.

A further example of how time does not heal on Truk
is that of a land dispute that started with the German
occupation in the 1890s, was carried on down through
the Japanese occupation, and was still current and acri-
monious when the Americans arrived in 1946.

Prior to Missionary Moses' arrival on Uman in 1867
life on Truk was characterized by violent and bloody
warfare. Villages, instead of being built on the shore
where life was a little easier, were placed on the sides of
mountains where they could be better protected. Attacks
would come without notice and often without apparent
provocation. Or a fight might start if a man stole a
coconut from a tree that was not his or waylaid a woman
and took advantage of her. Years later someone would
start thinking about the wrong and decide that it still had
not been righted. A village would be attacked again in
the middle of the night.

When charges were brought against a chief for things
he had done to his people, every little slight, every minor
graft would be listed; nothing would be forgotten. Dam-
ages would be asked for everything. It seemed preposter-
ous to us Americans, particularly when we looked at the
lists of charges. "How could a chief be so corrupt?" "How
could the people remember so much?"

Though the Truk islanders carry the accumulated burden of time past on their shoulders, they show an almost total inability to grasp the notion that two events can take place at the same time when they are any distance apart. When the Japanese occupied Truk at the end of World War I they took Artie Moses, chief of the island of Uman, to Tokyo. Artie was made to send a wireless message back to his people as a demonstration of the wisardry of Japanese technology. His family refused to believe that he had sent it, that he had said anything at all, though they knew he was in Tokyo. Places at a distance are very real to them, but people who are away are very much away, and any interaction with them is unthinkable.

An entirely different handling of time is reported by the anthropologist Paul Bohannan for the Tiv, a primitive people who live in Nigeria. Like the Navajo, they point to the sun to indicate a general time of day, and they also observe the movement of the moon as it waxes and wanes. What is different is the way they use and experience time. For the Tiv, time is like a capsule. There is a time for visiting, for cooking, or for working; and when one is in one of these times, one does not shift to another.

The Tiv equivalent of the week lasts five to seven days. It is not tied into periodic natural events, such as the phases of the moon. The day of the week is named after the things which are being sold in the nearest "market." If we had the equivalent, Monday would be "automobiles" in Washington, D.C., "furniture" in Baltimore, and "yard goods" in New York. Each of these might be followed by the days for appliances, liquor, and diamonds in the respective cities. This would mean that as you traveled about the day of the week would keep changing, depending on where you were.

A requisite of our own temporal system is that the components must add up: Sixty seconds have to equal one minute, sixty minutes one hour. The American is perplexed by people who do not do this. The African specialist Henri Alexandre Junod, reporting on the Thonga, tells of a medicine man who had memorized a seventy-year chronology and could detail the events of each and every year in sequence. Yet this same man spoke of the period he had memorized as an "era" which he computed at "four months and eight hundred years' duration." The usual reaction to this story and others like it is that the man was primitive, like a child, and did not understand what he was saying, because how could seventy years possibly be the same as eight hundred? As students of culture we can no longer dismiss other conceptualizations of reality by saying that they are childlike. We must go much deeper. In the case of the Thonga it seems that a "chronology" is one thing and an "era" something else quite different, and there is no relation between the two in operational terms.

If these distinctions between European-American time and other conceptions of time seem to draw too heavily on primitive peoples, let me mention two other examples—from cultures which are as civilized, if not as industrialized, as our own. In comparing the United States with Iran and Afghanistan very great differences in the handling of time appear. The American attitude toward appointments is an example. Once while in Tehran I had an opportunity to observe some young Iranians making plans for a party. After plans were made to pick up everyone at appointed times and places everything began to fall apart. People would leave messages that they were unable to take so-and-so or were going somewhere else, knowing full well that the person who had been given the message couldn't possibly deliver it. One young woman was left stranded on a street corner, and no one seemed to be concerned about it. One of my informants explained that he himself had had many

similar experiences. Once he had made eleven appointments to meet a friend. Each time one of them failed to
show up. The twelfth time they swore they would both
be there, that nothing would interfere. The friend failed
to arrive. After waiting for forty-five minutes my informant phoned his friend and found him still at home. The
following conversation is an approximation of what took
place:

"Is that you, Abdul?" "Yes." "Why aren't you here? I
thought we were to meet for sure." "Oh, but it was
raining," said Abdul with a sort of whining intonation
that is very common in Parsi.

If present appointments are treated rather cavalierly,
the past in Iran takes on a very great importance. People
look back on what they feel are the wonders of the past
and the great ages of Persian culture. Yet the future seems
to have little reality or certainty to it. Businessmen have
been known to invest hundreds of thousands of dollars in
factories of various sorts without making the slightest
plan as to how to use them. A complete woolen mill was
bought and shipped to Tehran before the buyer had
raised enough money to erect it, to buy supplies, or even
to train personnel. When American teams of technicians
came to help Iran's economy they constantly had to cope
with what seemed to them an almost total lack of planning.

Moving east from Iran to Afghanistan, one gets farther
afield from American time concepts. A few years ago in
Kabul a man appeared, looking for his brother. He asked
all the merchants of the market place if they had seen his
brother and told them where he was staying in case his
brother arrived and wanted to find him. The next year he
was back and repeated the performance. By this time one
of the members of the American embassy had heard
about his inquiries and asked if he had found his brother.

The man answered that he and his brother had agreed to meet in Kabul, but neither of them had said what year.

Strange as some of these stories about the ways in which people handle time may seem, they become understandable when they are correctly analyzed. To do this adequately requires an adequate theory of culture. Before we return to the subject of time again—in a much later chapter of this book—I hope that I will have provided just such a theory. It will not only shed light on the way time is meshed with many other aspects of society but will provide a key to unlock some of the secrets of the eloquent language of culture which speaks in so many different ways.

2

WHAT IS CULTURE?

Culture is a word that has so many meanings already that one more can do it no harm. Before this book is finished I will redefine it again—in such a way, I hope, as to clarify what has become a very muddied concept. For anthropologists culture has long stood for the way of life of a people, for the sum of their learned behavior patterns, attitudes, and material things. Though they subscribe to this general view, most anthropologists tend to disagree however, on what the precise substance of culture is. In practice their work often leads some of them to a fascination with a single category of events among the many which make up human life, and they tend to think of this as the essence of all culture. Others, looking for a point of stability in the flux of society, often become preoccupied with identifying a common particle or element which can be found in every aspect of culture. In sum, though the concept of culture was first defined in print in 1871 by E. B. Tylor, after all these years it still lacks the rigorous specificity which characterizes many less revolutionary and useful ideas.

Even more unfortunate is the slowness with which the concept of culture has percolated through the public consciousness. Compared to such notions as the unconscious or repression, to use two examples from psychology, the idea of culture is a strange one even to the informed citizen. The reasons for this are well worth noting, for they suggest some of the difficulties which are inherent in the culture concept itself.

From the beginning, culture has been the special province of the anthropologist, who usually gained a firsthand experience of its pervasive power in the field during the internship which follows the prescribed period of classroom training. As fledgling anthropologists moved deeper and deeper into the life of the people they were studying they inevitably acquired the conviction that culture was real and not just something dreamed up by the theoretician. Moreover, as they slowly mastered the complexities of a given culture they were apt to feel that these complexities could be understood in no other way than by prolonged experience, and that it was almost impossible to communicate this understanding to anyone who had not lived through the same experience.

This frame of mind alone would have been enough to isolate the growing skills of the anthropologists from the everyday society about them which might have well used their special insights and knowledge. But there were other reasons too. What technical training the anthropologists had was rather lengthy and detailed. It concerned subjects which seemed to have little relevance to the problems of the layman engrossed in his/her own society. Moreover, until the last war few Americans had even heard of the places the anthropologists frequented or the people they studied, who were generally small isolated populations with little place in the power politics of the modern world. There seemed to be no "practical" value attached to either what the anthropologist did or what they made of their discoveries. Except for a certain curiosity or nostalgia which might be satisfied, what point was there in studying the American Indian, who was usually viewed as the romantic red man, a remnant of the days long gone, or as an embarrassing reminder that there had been a time when Americans were ruthless with those who stood in the way of progress? Despite an occasional flurry of popular interest, anthropology (and the culture concept which is at its heart) was long associated in people's minds with subject matter and individuals who are far removed from the realities of the everyday world of business and politics. Though it still persists in some quarters, this viewpoint was at its strongest up until the time of the early 1930s.

The depression changed many things. It led to the peaceful introduction of many ideas which had been considered revolutionary. One was the application of social science theory and techniques to the mundane problems of the nation's domestic economy. Anthropologists, for example, were suddenly called from their academic refuge and put to work trying to relieve some of the more pressing burdens of the nation's minority groups.

Among this long-suffering population were the Indians, living miserably depressed lives on reservations as wards of the government. Most of these Indians had neither the dignity of their old ways nor the advantages of the now dominant society that surrounded them. Up to this point it had been the government's policy to treat all the different tribes alike, as if they were ignorant and somewhat stubborn children—a mistake which is yet to be really rectified. A body of custom had grown up in the government's Indian Service as to how to "handle" Indians and Indian problems. Like the State Department's Foreign Service, the Indian Service transferred its employees from post to post so often that they could put in a lifetime of service without learning anything about the people they were administering. The bureaucracy that grew up was more oriented toward the problems of the employees than those of the Indians. Under such conditions it was almost impossible to introduce the disturbing anthropological idea that the Indians were deeply and significantly different from European-Americans, for that would have threatened to upset the bureaucratic apple-cart. Though the treatment of the Indians by the government still leaves much to be desired, it has been vastly improved during the years in which trained anthropologists have worked on the reservations.

In World War II many anthropologists such as myself were not only put to work on various projects having to do with the natives of the Southwest Pacific but were even asked to deal with the Japanese. Under the pressure of war some of the advice we gave was heeded—though, like many wartime innovations, much that was done was forgotten in the peace that followed.

However, the field work which anthropologists did as pure research, plus the applied projects on which we worked, was not entirely wasted. If this rich experience taught us one thing it was that culture is more than mere custom that can be shed or changed like a suit of clothes. The people we were advising kept bumping their heads against an invisible barrier, but they did not know what it was. We knew that what they were up against was a completely different way of organizing life, of thinking, and of conceiving the underlying assumptions about the family and the state, the economic system, and even of mankind. The big problem was how to communicate this brute fact. When we tried to point it out our explanations didn't make sense. Most of our attempts were anecdotal and very little was specific.

Apart from having problems with laymen who often did not really care about a definition of culture, we had certain methodological difficulties in the field itself. The most pressing one was consistency of basic information. Field workers would record their interpretations of what informants told them, but if someone else visited the same group and interviewed a different set of informants or even the same informants (a practice frowned upon by anthropologists) the second man would usually come back with a different set of interpretations. There was no way to gather data that could be legitimately checked, no way to reproduce field procedures, no way to equate an event in culture A with culture B except to try to describe each and they say that they were different. It was difficult, if not impossible, to say in precise terms what it was that made one culture really different from another, except to point out that there were people who raised sheep and others who gathered food; that there were those who hunted and those who cultivated plants; that people worshiped different gods and organized their societies in varying ways. The anthropologist knew that there were even more profound differences, but his readers and often the very officials he was advising preferred to ignore them. Without being quite aware of it these well-meaning gentlemen assumed a naïvely evolutionary view which classified most foreigners as "underdeveloped Americans."

Even now, when the populations of the so-called "underdeveloped" areas balk at the introduction of new techniques of health and agriculture by the Americans, they are thought to be backward and stubborn, or thought to be led by greedy leaders who have no concern for their people's welfare. Leaders were usually blamed and sometimes even accused of coercing their people to resist innovation because it would break their strangle hold on the economy.

Unfortunately some of these things are true, and they offer a convenient excuse for this country's failures abroad on the technical assistance, military aid, and diplomatic fronts. Most of our difficulties stem from our own ignorance. Honest and sincere people in the field continue to fail to grasp the true significance of the fact that culture controls behavior in deep and persisting ways, many of which are outside of awareness and therefore beyond conscious control of the individual. When anthropologists stress this point they are usually ignored, for they are challenging the deepest popular American beliefs about ourselves as well as foreigners. They lead people to see things they might not want to see.

Moreover, as I have pointed out, the solemn strictures of the anthropologist to the layman who might make use of these insights lack the necessary concreteness. There is no way to *teach* culture in the same way that language is taught. Until recently no one had defined any basic units of culture. There was no generally agreed upon underlying theory of culture—no way of being specific— no way for B to get to the field and check A's results. Even today a volume examining the various concepts and theories of culture, written by the nation's two most distinguished anthropologists, A. L. Kroeber and Clyde Kluckhohn, calls for such qualities as "empathy" in the investigator. The authors also state that no constant elemental units of culture have as yet been satisfactorily established.

This state of affairs had been a source of irritation for a number of years, and it drove me to work toward an integrated theory of culture which would overcome the shortcomings I have just sketched. In 1951, when I came to Washington to train Point Four technicians, I had a very practical reason for pressing this work toward a tangible conclusion. Prior to this time I had been teaching at a university and a small college. College students are content to take subjects for their general interest. Point Four technicians and Foreign Service officers, on the other hand, are expected to go overseas and get results, and they have to be well prepared. In general I found that they are not too interested in the anthropologist's preoccupation with "what culture is" and tend to become impatient unless they have been abroad previously and have had some actual experience. Foreign Service officers in particular used to take great delight in saying that what the anthropologists told them about working with the Navajo didn't do them much good, for we didn't have an embassy on the Navajo reservation. Unfortunately the theory we were able to bring to bear at the time I began working in Washington simply had no perceived relevance to the operator in the field. Their defenses were too well entrenched and we could show them no compelling reasons to change. Additional harassment came from the government administrators who failed to grasp the fact that there was something really different about overseas operation; that what was needed was something bold and new, not just more of the same old history, economics, and politics.

Those Foreign Service officers and other trainees who did take seriously what they heard and managed to make something out of it came up against another problem. They would say, "Yes, I can see that you have something there. Now I'm going to Damascus. Where can I read something that will help me to do business with the Arabs?" We were stumped! If they were going to Japan we could tell them to read Ruth Benedict's excellent book, *The Chrysanthemum and the Sword*, with the caution that it was for background only and they shouldn't expect to find conditions exactly like those that Benedict described. Of course the remarkable thing about Benedict's book was that, while she had never been to Japan and could only work with Japanese who were in the United States (the book was written during the war), it showed extraordinary insight into the psychological processes of the

Japanese. It is one of the best pieces of evidence that the anthropologist has something crucial and practical to say if it can only be systematized.

Just about this time George L. Trager and I began our collaboration to develop a method for the analysis of culture. Our ultimate objectives included five basic steps.

1. To identify the building blocks of culture—what we later came to call the *isolates* of culture, akin to the notes in a musical score.

2. To tie these isolates into a biological base so that they could be compared among cultures. We also stipulated that this comparison be done in such a way that the conditions be repeatable at will. Without this, anthropology can lay no claim to being a science.

3. To build up a body of data and a methodology that would enable us to conduct research and teach each cultural situation in much the same way that language is taught without having to depend upon such qualities as "empathy" in the researcher.

4. To build a unified theory of culture that would lead us to further research.

5. Finally, to find a way to make our discipline tangibly useful to the non-specialist.

Trager and I felt that much of the preoccupation of anthropologists with statistics was having a stultifying effect on our discipline and that the methodologies and theories borrowed from sociology, psychology, and other biological and physical sciences had been ineptly used. In many instances social scientists, under pressure from physical scientists, have been virtually panicked into adopting prematurely the rigors of formal mathematics and the "scientific method." Our view was that it was necessary for anthropology to develop its own methodology adapted to its own subject matter.

This book outlines both a theory of culture and a

theory of how culture came into being. It treats culture in its entirety as a form of communication.

It sketches in the biological roots from which most if not all of culture grew and outlines the ten basic foci of activity that combine to produce culture. Chapters Three and Four describe how humans experience things on three different levels, how they communicate to their children in three ways while in the process of rearing them, how they alternate between three different types of awareness or consciousness and embue each experience with three different types of emotional overtones. I have called this crucial trio the *formal, informal,* and *technical.* An understanding of what these terms mean is basic to an understanding of the rest of the book. Since humans progress from formal belief to informal adaptation and finally to technical analysis, a theory of change is also implied in this tripartite division which is at the heart of my theory.

The next chapters (Five through Eight) specify and deal with the communication spectrum. Little is said about mass-communication media such as the press, radio, and television, which are the instruments used to extend people's senses. Rather these chapters are focused on one main aspect of communication, the ways in which people read meaning into what others do. Language is the most technical of the message systems. It is used as a model for the analysis of the others. In addition to language there are other ways in which people communicate that either reinforce or deny what they have said with words. People learn to read different segments of a communication spectrum covering events of a fraction of a second up to events of many years. This book deals with only a small part of this spectrum. Other chapters describe the content of messages of the man-to-man variety and how they are put together.

The final chapters are a more detailed analysis of time and space. Time, that silent language which was sketched so broadly in the first chapter, is analyzed in more detail as an example of one of the types of primary message systems. Chapter Eleven deals with space (territoriality) as communication.

If this book has a message it is that we must learn to understand the "out-of-awareness" aspects of communication. We must never assume that we are fully aware of what we communicate to someone else. There exists in the world today tremendous distortions in meaning as men try to communicate with one another. The job of achieving understanding and insight into mental processes of others is much more difficult and the situation more serious than most of us care to admit.

Up to this point I have talked primarily of problems that have grown out of attempts to teach others to apply anthropological knowledge to foreign relations. I have also emphasized the need for more systematic understanding of local culture on the part of our citizens who are working abroad. The average reader who hasn't lived abroad, who finds the work of the diplomat and the Point Four technician exceedingly remote, may be inclined to ask, "What's this got to do with me?" This point touches on the ultimate purpose of this book, which is to reveal the broad extent to which culture controls our lives. Culture is not an exotic notion studied by a select group of anthropologists in the South Seas. It is a mold in which we are all cast, and it controls our daily lives in many unsuspected ways. In my discussion of culture I will be describing that part of human behavior which we take for granted—the part we don't think about, since we assume it is universal or regard it as idiosyncratic.

Culture hides much more than it reveals, and strangely enough what it hides, it hides most effectively from its own participants. Years of study have convinced me that the real job is not to understand foreign culture but to understand our own. I am also convinced that all that one ever gets from studying foreign culture is a token understanding. The ultimate reason for such study is to learn more about how one's own system works. The best reason for exposing oneself to foreign ways is to generate a sense of vitality and awareness—an interest in life which can come only when one lives through the shock of contrast and difference.

Simply learning one's own culture is an achievement of gargantuan proportions for anyone. By the age of twenty-five or thirty most of us have finished school, been married, learned to live with another human being, mastered a job, seen the miracle of human birth, and started a new human being well on his way to growing up. Suddenly most of what we have to learn is finished. Life begins to settle down.

Yet our tremendous brain has endowed us with a drive and a capacity for learning which appear to be as strong as the drive for food or sex. This means that when a middle-aged man or woman stops learning he or she is often left with a great drive and highly developed capacities. If this individual goes to live in another culture, the learning process is often reactivated. For most Americans tied down at home this is not possible. To forestall atrophy of their intellectual powers people can begin learning about those areas of their own culture which have been out of awareness. They can explore the new frontier.

The problem which is raised in talking about American culture without reference to other cultures is that an audience tends to take the remarks personally. I once addressed a group of school principals on the subject of culture. We were discussing the need for Americans to progress in their jobs, to get ahead, and to receive some recognition so that they would know in a tangible way that they were actually getting someplace. One of the audience said to me, "Now you are talking about something interesting, you're talking about me." When the man in the audience learned something about himself, the study of culture got lost in the shuffle. He did not seem to realize that a significant proportion of the material which was highly personal to him was also relevant cultural data.

A knowledge of his own culture would have helped this same man in a situation which he subsequently described for the audience. In the middle of a busy day, it seems, his son had kept him waiting for an hour. As a result he was aware that his blood pressure had risen rather dangerously. If both the father and the son had had a cultural perspective on this common and infuriating occurrence the awkward quarrel which followed might have been avoided. Both father and son would have benefited if the father had understood the cultural basis of his tension and explained, "Now, look here. If you want to keep me waiting, O.K., but you should know it is a real slap in the face to anyone to be kept waiting so long. If that's what you want to communicate, go ahead, but be sure you know that you are communicating an insult and don't act like a startled fawn if people react accordingly."

The best reason for the layperson to spend time studying culture is that he/she can learn something useful and enlightening about himself/herself. This can be an interesting process, at times harrowing but ultimately rewarding. One of the most effective ways to learn about oneself is by taking seriously the cultures of others. It forces you to pay attention to those details of life which differentiate them from you.

For those who are familiar with the subject the remarks I have just made should be a clear indication that what follows is not simply a rehash of what previous writers on the subject of culture have said. The approach is new. It involves new ways of looking at things. Indians and natives of the South Pacific, the hallmarks of most anthropological texts, are used. However, they are introduced solely to clarify points about our own way of life, to make what we take for granted stand out in perspective. Some of what appears between these covers has been presented before in short articles in technical journals by either Trager or myself. Most of it is presented to the public for the first time. The complete theory of culture as communication is new and has not been presented in one place before. If the reader is looking for a book on strange customs, they will be sorely disappointed. This book stresses more than anything else, not what people talk about, but what people do and the hidden rules that govern people.

Some of what follows will make readers self-conscious. They will discover that they are conveying to others things they never dreamed they were revealing. In some instances they will learn things they have been hiding from themselves. The language of culture speaks as clearly as the language of dreams Freud analyzed, but, unlike dreams, it cannot be kept to oneself. When I talk about culture I am not just talking about something in the abstract that is imposed on mankind and is separate from individuals, but about humans themselves, about you and me in a highly personal way.

3

THE VOCABULARY OF CULTURE

Sir Arthur Conan Doyle's success with his creation, Sherlock Holmes, is largely attributable to the fact that Holmes knew how to make the most of non-verbal communication and extracted the maximum from what he observed. The following excerpt from "A Case of Identity" aptly illustrates this point.

He had risen from his chair and was standing between the parted blinds, gazing down into the dull neutral-tinted London street. Looking over his shoulder, I saw that on the pavement opposite there stood a large woman with a heavy fur boa around her neck, and a large curling red feather in a broad-brimmed hat which was tilted in a coquettish Duchess of Devonshire fashion over her ear. From under this great panoply she peeped up in a nervous, hesitating fashion at our windows, while her body oscillated backward and forward, and her fingers fidgeted with her glove buttons. Suddenly, with a plunge, as of the swimmer who leaves the bank, she hurried across the road and we heard the sharp clang of the bell.

"I have seen those symptoms before," said Holmes, throw-

ing his cigarette into the fire. "Oscillation upon the pavement always means an *affaire de coeur*. She would like advice,
but is not sure that the matter is not too delicate for
communication. And yet even here we may discriminate.
When a woman has been seriously wronged by a man she
no longer oscillates, and the usual symptom is a broken bell
wire. Here we may take it that there is a love matter, but
that the maiden is not so much angry as perplexed, or
grieved. But here she comes in person to resolve our
doubts."

Sir Arthur made explicit a highly complex process
which many of us go through without knowing that we
are involved. Those of us who keep our eyes open can
read volumes into what we see going on around us.
During the first half of this century, the citizens of a
typical American farming community, for example, did
not have to be told why old Mr. Jones was going to town.
They knew that every other Thursday he made a trip to
the druggist to get his wife a bottle of tonic and that
after that he went around to the feed store, visited with
Charley, dropped in to call on the sheriff, and then went
home in time for the noonday meal. Jones, in turn, could
also tell whenever anything was bothering one of his
friends, and the chances are that he would be able to
figure out precisely what it was. He felt comfortable in
his way of life because most of the time he "knew what
the score was." He didn't have to say much to get his
point across; a nod of the head or a grunt as he left the
store was sufficient. People took him as he was. On the
other hand, strangers disturbed him, not because their
mannerisms were different, but because he knew so little
about them. When Jones met a stranger, communication,
which was normally as natural as breathing, suddenly
became difficult and overly complex.

Most of us move around so much these days that we
seldom achieve that comfortable stage that Jones has

reached with his cronies—though there are always enough familiar landmarks around so that we are never at a total loss for orientation. Yet in many cases people who move from one part of the country to another require several years before they are really worked into the new area and feel completely at ease. Not only do Americans engage in a constant internal migration, but a million and a half of us are living overseas in foreign surroundings and the number is increasing each year. Jones's anxieties when he meets an unfamiliar person or environment are trivial compared to what our overseas travelers go through when they land on foreign soil. At first, things in the cities look pretty much alike. There are taxis, hotels with hot and cold running water, theaters, neon lights, even tall buildings with elevators and a few people who speak English. But pretty soon the American discovers that underneath the familiar exterior there are vast differences. When someone says "yes" it often doesn't mean yes at all, and when people smile it doesn't always mean that they are pleased. When American visitors make a helpful gesture they may be rebuffed; when they try to be friendly nothing happens. People tell them they will do things and don't. The longer they stay, the more enigmatic the new country looks, until finally they begin to learn to observe new cues that reinforce or negate the words people are saying with their mouths. They discover that even Sherlock Holmes would be helpless in a country so different as Japan and that only his Japanese counterpart could play such a role.

At this point Americans abroad may either burst with exasperation and try to withdraw as much as they can from the foreign life about them or begin to wonder, rather shrewdly, about what they must do to escape a frustrating comedy of errors. If they are charitable they may even begin to reflect on how they can help a new arrival avoid the wearing experience of doing all the wrong things. This can be the beginning of a cultural wisdom, for it leads to systematic thinking about the learning process which nearly everyone goes through as they become familiar with a new culture.

In pursuing this problem of how one culture differs from another and how one can communicate this difference in general terms I first decided that there was no single touchstone which could be used to explain any given culture. In this I found myself in disagreement with many anthropologists who look upon culture as a single category. I was led to my conclusion by the realization that there is no break between the present, in which humans act as culture-producing animals, and the past, when there were no "people" and no cultures. There is an unbroken continuity between the far past and the present, for culture is bio-basic—rooted in biological activities. Infra-culture is the term which can be given to behavior that preceded culture but later became elaborated by humans into culture as we know it today. Territoriality is an example of an infra-cultural activity. It has to do with the way in which territory is claimed and defended by everything from fish to lions to modern humans.

By going back to infra-culture it is possible to demonstrate that the complex bases—mainly biological—upon which human behavior have been built were laid down at different times in the history of evolution. Trager and I also reasoned that the number of infra-cultural bases were probably very few and that they probably led to very different type of activities, things that on the surface bore little or no apparent relationship to each other.

Since culture is learned, it also seemed clear that one should be able to teach it. Yet in the past there had been singularly little success in this regard with the important exception of language, one of the dominant threads in all cultures. The answer to this question is rooted in understanding the difference between acquisition and learning. Most of culture is acquired and therefore cannot be taught. Since language is first acquired at an early age and later taught, it was the dramatic progress in teaching, analyzing, and working with language made possible by modern linguistic science prompted us to take a very careful look at how this success had been achieved. Our observations led to the establishment of criteria for other systems of culture. In order to qualify as a cultural system, each system had to be:

A. Rooted in a biological activity widely shared with other advanced living forms. It was essential that there be no breaks with the past.

B. Capable of analysis in its own terms without reference to the other systems and so organized that it contained isolated components that could be built up into more complex units, and paradoxically—

C. So constituted that it reflected all the rest of culture and was reflected in the rest of culture.

These criteria are operational. That is, they are based on direct observation of the actual functioning of a cultural system, in this case language. The criteria, from an anthropological point of view, are firm. There are ten separate kinds of human activity which I have labeled Primary Message Systems (PMS). Only the first PMS involves language. All the other PMS are non-linguistic forms of the communication process. Since each is enmeshed in the others, one can start the study of culture with any one of the ten and eventually come out with a complete picture. The Primary Message Systems are:

1. Interaction
2. Association
3. Subsistence
4. Bisexuality
5. Territoriality
6. Temporality

7. Learning
8. Play
9. Defense
10. Exploitation (use of materials)

In discussing the PMS one by one I will stress three things: How biology prevades each PMS, how each can be examined by itself, and how each gears into the over-all network of culture.

1. *Interaction* has its basis in the underlying irritability of all living substance. To interact with the environment is to be alive, and to fail to do so is to be dead. Beginning with the basic irritability of the simplest life forms, interaction patterns become more complex as they ascend the philogenetic scale.

One of the most highly elaborated forms of interaction is speech, which is reinforced by tone of voice and gesture. Writing is a special form of interaction which uses a particular set of symbols and specially developed forms. In addition to the well-known linguistic interaction there are specialized versions for each PMS. People interact with others as a function of living in groups (association). Time and space are dimensions in which interaction takes place. Teaching, learning, play, and defense also represent specialized forms of interaction.

Ultimately everything people do involves interaction with something else. Interaction lies at the hub of the universe of culture and everything grows from it.

2. *Association*. It is easy to forget that the bodies of complex organisms are in reality societies of cells, most of which have highly specialized functions, and that the first associations along this line were between cells that banded together in colonies. Association, therefore, be-gins when two cells have joined.

Years ago psychologists attracted considerable attention with their descriptions of the "pecking order" of chickens. It will be remembered that in each flock there is always one chicken that pecks all the others but does not get pecked by any others, and at the bottom there is one that gets pecked by all the rest. Between the extremes the flock is arranged in an orderly progression ranging from the one that is second from the bottom and has only one chicken it can peck, up to the #2 bird, who is pecked only by the leader. As it happens, all living things arrange their lives in some sort of recognizable pattern of *association*. Chickens have a peck order, horses a "kick-bite" order. In some cases a rigidly ordered hierarchy is replaced by another form of association. Konrad Lorenz describes two different patterns of association in his descriptions of dogs. These patterns are based on the ancestral behavior of wolves and jackals. The wolves have a very highly developed loyalty to the pack as well as to the leader, which is established early and persists through life. Jackals, on the other hand, seem to form much more loosely knit associations that are situational in character. They do not have the loyalty of the wolf either to the leader or to the pack. They are much more fickle, quicker to make friends, and less loyal over the long haul.

Other forms of association can be seen in flocks of sheep, herds of deer or cattle, schools of fish, paired relationships of some birds and mammals like the lion and the goose, and the family of the gorilla. Associational patterns persist over long periods of time, and if they change at all it is because of very strong pressure from the environment. The famous anthropologist, Ralph Linton, pointed out that lions in Kenya used to hunt singly or in pairs. When game became scarce they took up hunting in packs. The interesting thing is that each lion had a function associated with his role in the group. The procedure was for the lions to form a large circle, leaving one of their number in the center. By roaring and closing in they would drive the game toward the middle, where it could be killed by the single lion. Changes in association of this sort anticipate the kind of adaptive behavior humans exhibit.

Human elaborations on the simpler mammalian base are so complex and varied that only their grosser outlines have been analyzed and described. What I am dealing with here are the various ways in which societies and their components are organized or structured.

The interrelation of the PMS of association and language is exemplified in the varieties of dialects of social classes. Other examples: the tone of voice of a person when he or she is acting as a leader; the very special elaboration of status and deference forms developed by the Japanese to fit their highly structured hierarchies; in our own society the deferential ways of talking to individuals who are ranked higher in work or status situations (nurses to doctors, privates to captains, captains to generals, etc.).

3. *Subsistence.* Like the other PMS, subsistence is basic and dates back to the very beginning of life. One of the first things anyone has to know about any living thing is its nutritional requirements; what does it eat and how does it go about getting food in its natural state? Humans have elaborated this matter of feeding themselves, working, and making a living in the same way they have elaborated the other PMS. Included in the PMS of subsistence is everything from individual food habits to the economy of a country. Not only are people classified and dealt with in terms of diet, but each society has its own characteristic economy.

In regard to the relationship of subsistence to the other PMS, one has only to mention such things as the special language behavior at meals. There are strict taboos covering discussion at the table of topics such as sex or the bodily functions. Then there are the special vocabulary and usage that have grown up around each occupation and profession, each a highly specialized form of subsistence. Work is of course always ranked, fitting very closely into the existing patterns of association. What is ranked high in one culture, however, may be ranked very low in the next. This is one of the many points which constantly confront Americans abroad, whether they are in a government technical assistance program, an industrial operation, or traveling as tourists.

Americans attach no stigma to work with the hands, but in many other cultures manual labor is considered to be undignified, a sign of low status. This difference alone creates innumerable difficulties and delays. Sometimes the role of the American is misinterpreted when they "pitch in" or demonstrate how something is to be done. On other occasions the local nationals simply refuse to have anything to do with an occupation that is ranked so low that it has to be done with the hands. For years throughout Latin America nursing was retarded because it ranked so near the bottom of the scale that only uneducated girls would become nurses. The handling of bedpans as well as many other duties normally linked with nursing were considered menial and dirty. Similarly, attempts to teach industrial safety in Latin America foundered on cultural reefs when it was discovered that safety engineers had to wear coveralls and "demonstrate" safety measures on machines in the plant.

4. *Bisexuality.* Sexual reproduction and differentiation of both form and function along sex lines (bisexuality) is also deeply rooted in the past. Its primary function can best be explained in terms of a need to supply a variety of combinations of genetic background as a means of meeting changes in the environment. Without sex, progeny follow only one line and maintain one set of characteristics. In humans the combinations of genes are practically unlimited.

People who have had anything to do with animals know how basic sexual differences are within a species.

One of the first things that must be known about an animal is whether it is the male or female of the species. The fact that behavior in animals is predominately sex-linked has led to certain misconceptions concerning the role of sex in humans. It is a great mistake to assume that the behavior which is observed in people is linked to physiology. Studies of culture have shown us that this is usually not the case. Behavior that is exhibited by males in one culture may be classed as feminine in another. All cultures differentiate between men and women, and usually when a given behavior pattern becomes associated with one sex it will be dropped by the other.

In much of Latin America it was long thought that a man could not possibly suppress the strong urges that took possession of him every time he was alone with a woman. In the eyes of Latinos, women were considered unable to resist a man. The result was that the patterns of association contained safeguards and protective measures. Americans who were going to Latin America had to be cautioned that if they let themselves get into a situation with a member of the opposite sex where something could have happened, it would be no use to tell people that it had not. The Latin response would be, "After all, you're a man, aren't you? She's a woman, isn't she?" The point the Americans couldn't get through their heads was that these people really considered that men and women were constituted differently from the way the American views them. In Latin America both sexes expect their will power to be provided by other people rather than by personal inhibition.

In Iran one encounters another variation of the PMS of bisexuality. Men are expected to show their emotions—take Premier (1951–1953) Mossadegh's tantrums. If they don't, Iranians suspect they are lacking a vital human trait and are not dependable. Iranian men read poetry; they are sensitive and have well-developed intuition and in many cases are not expected to be too logical. They are often seen embracing and holding hands. Women, on the other hand, are considered to be coldly practical. They exhibit many of the characteristics associated with men in the United States. A very perceptive Foreign Service officer who had spent a number of years in Iran once observed, "If you will think of the emotional and intellectual sex roles as reversed from ours, you will do much better out here."

Remarks like this come as a shock to many people, because almost everyone has difficulty believing that behavior they have always associated with "human nature" is not human nature at all but learned behavior of a particularly complex variety. Possibly one of the many reasons why the culture concept has been resisted is that it throws doubts on many established beliefs. Fundamental beliefs like our concepts of masculinity and femininity ar shown to vary widely from one culture to the next. It is easier to avoid the idea of the culture concept than to face up to it.

Speech and sex are linked in obvious ways. Let the reader, if he or she doubts this, start talking like a member of the opposite sex for a while and see how long people let him or her get away with it. Sex and territory are also intermingled. For many birds there are breeding grounds, nesting territories, and, for many species, areas defended by males against other males. For humans there are places where the behavior of the sexes toward each other is prescribed, like the parlor or the bedroom. We can see an intermingling of sex and territory in pool halls or in the old-time saloon from which "ladies" were excluded.

Time also enters the picture, dating back to the era when there were mating seasons for many species. Humans, having freed themselves from the limitations formerly imposed by biology, have burdened themselves with many more, including those having to do with the determination of the age at which heterosexual relations are supposed to begin. Malinowski, when he described the Trobriand Islanders, told how the sex life of the Trobriander is usually in full progress at the ages of six to eight for girls and ten to twelve for boys.

5. *Territoriality.* Territoriality is the technical term used by the ethologist to describe the taking possession, use, and defense of a territory on the part of living organisms. Birds have recognizable territories in which they feed and nest; carnivorous animals have areas in which they hunt; bees have places in which they search for honey, and people use space for all the activities in which they engage. The balance of life in the use of space is one of the most delicate of nature. Territoriality reaches into every nook and cranny of life. When they are in the ring, even the fighting bulls of Spain are likely to establish safe territories from which it is difficult to get them to move.

The history of mankind's past is largely an account of our efforts to wrest space from others and to defend space from outsiders. A quick review of the map of Europe over the past half century reflects this fact. A multitude of familiar examples can be found to illustrate the idea of human territoriality. Beggars have beats, as do the policemen who try to get them to leave, and prostitutes work their own side of the street. Salesmen and distributors have their own territories which they will defend like any other living organism. The symbolism of the phrase "to move in on someone" is completely accurate and appropriate. To have a territory is to have one of the essential components of life; to lack one is one of the most precarious of all conditions.

Space (or territoriality) meshes very subtly with the rest of culture in many different ways. Status, for example, is indicated by the distance one sits from the head of the table on formal occasions; shifts take place in the voice as one increases the distance (whispering to shouting); there are *areas* for work, play, education, and defense; and there are instruments such as rulers, chains, and range finders for measuring space and boundaries for everything from a house to a state.

6. *Temporality*. Temporality, as I have pointed out in the past chapter, is tied into life in so many ways that it is difficult to ignore it. Life is full of cycles and rhythms, some of them related directly to nature—the respiration rate, heartbeat, menstrual cycle, and so on. Such practices as age-grading (dividing society according to rather rigid age groups) combine both time and association. Mealtimes, of course, vary from culture to culture, as do tempos of speech. It should be mentioned that there are students of culture who look at everything as a historical process, and there can be no doubt that if you know the temporal relationships between events you know a tremendous amount.

7. *Learning and Acquisition*. Learning and acquisition are different processes. Recent insights based on observation of children *acquiring* language *on their own* reveal that this type of modification of behavior also occurs for all of the rest of basic culture. The process assumed primary importance as an adaptive mechanism when common ancestors of birds and mammals became warm-blooded at some time either late in the Permian or early Triassic periods, over 100,000,000 years ago.

Before this time all life's tempo was tied to the temperature of the external environment. As the temperature dropped, movement slowed down. This did not represent a disadvantage to any given species when all were cold-blooded, because everything slowed down together. With the internalization of temperature controls, the warm-blooded animals were freed from the restrictions imposed upon them by the fluctuations in external temperature. This endowed them with a tremendously enhanced survival value, enhanced sensory perceptions, and at the same time placed a premium on adaptations—such as migrations, nests, lairs, etc.—that enabled the organism to cope with temperature extremes.

One result of warm-bloodedness is that it imposes on the organism a minimal size below which it cannot fall since it would perish of heat loss. When body size falls below a certain minimum the increased surface in relation to volume is such that the animal cannot eat fast enough to keep its metabolic fires going. It has been established that a *fat* hummingbird can fly 7.7 hours before its reserve of fat (1 gram) is consumed. Thin ones would fare less well, while some shrews apparently will die of starvation in a few hours.

With the increase in size associated with warm-bloodedness, a ceiling is set on numbers. Birds, mammals, and insects have all demonstrated high aptitude for adaptation to environmental changes. The insect kingdom compensated for the short life span of its members by breeding in enormous numbers. Warm-blooded animals obviously needed some other adaptive technique because of their great size, long life, and relatively small numbers of offspring. They grew to depend more and more on acquisition and later learning as an adaptive device. However, true learning really came into its own as an adaptive mechanism when it could be *extended in time and space by means of language*. A fawn can learn about people with guns by the reaction of its mother when a person with a gun appears, but there is no possible way, lacking language, for that fawn to be forewarned in the absence of an actual demonstration. Animals have no way of symbolically *storing* their learning against future needs.

Psychologists of late have been preoccupied with learning theory, and one anthropologist, John Gillin, has worked learning theory into his text on anthropology.

What complicates matters, however, is that people reared in different cultures *learn to learn* differently and go about the process of acquiring culture in their own way. Some do so by memory and rote without reference to "logic" as we think of it, while some learn by demonstration but without the teacher requiring the student to do anything himself while "learning." Some cultures, like the American, stress doing as a principle of learning, while others have very little of the pragmatic. The Japanese even guide the hand of the pupil, while our teachers usually aren't permitted to touch the other person. Education and educational systems are about as laden with emotion and as characteristic of a given culture as its language. It should not come as a surprise that we encounter real opposition to our educational system when we make attempts to transfer it overseas.

Learning to learn differently is something that has to be faced every day by people who go overseas and try to train local personnel. It seems inconceivable to the average person brought up in one culture that something as basic as this could be done any differently from the way they themselves were taught. The fact is, however, that once people have learned to learn in a given way it is extremely hard for them to learn in any other way. This is because, in the process of learning they have *acquired* a long set of tacit conditions and assumptions in which learning is imbedded.

The rest of culture reflects the way one learns, since culture is "learned and shared behavior." Learning, then, is one of the basic activities of life, and educators might have a better grasp of their art if they would take a leaf out of the book of the early pioneers in descriptive linguistics and learn about their subject by studying the acquired context in which other people learn. Men like Sapir revolutionized linguistic theory and ultimately language-teaching methods as the direct consequence of their having to deal with problems that arose from studying the "primitive" languages. The so-called "army method" of World War II was deeply influenced by anthropologically trained linguistic scientists. So was the current State Department language program.

The educator has much to learn about his own systems of learning by immersing himself in those that are so different that they raise questions that have never been raised before. Americans in particular have too long assumed that the U.S. educational system represents the ultimate in evolution and that other systems are less advanced than our own. Even the highly elaborated and beautifully adapted educational techniques of Japan, in which the acquired base is entirely different from our own, have been looked down upon. Just why we feel so complacent and smug can be explained only by the blindness that culture imposes on its members. Certainly there is very little reason for complacency when one looks, not at others, but at ourselves. The fact that so many of our children dislike school or finish their schooling uneducated suggests that we still have much to learn about learning as a process. It also suggests that a deep chasm exists that separates the acquired side of American culture from the learned side.

As one watches one's own children grow up and learn, one reflects upon the vital role of learning as an agent of culture, to say nothing of its strategic place in the mechanism of survival. Any child, from the time it is born, without culture, until the time it is four or five, absorbs what goes on around it at a rate which is never equaled again in its lifetime. At six to ten children are still going strong, provided that the educational system hasn't produced blocks to learning.

Yet the schools are not the only agents responsible for education. Parents and older people in general play a part. Having learned to learn in a particular fashion, adults can communicate their prejudices or convictions in a variety of subtle and often not so subtle ways. Here is an example of this which has been experienced in one way or another by almost everyone who shares in our culture.

This story begins when a great-grandmother visits her three-year-old great-granddaughter. The child, like most three-year-olds, is toddling around and absorbing everything that's going on. Apart from eating and sleeping, one of her main concerns is to gain control of the communications taking place around her in order to be able to interact with others on their own terms. She is in the process of acquiring the base on which learned culture will later be built. Great-grandmother watches this. Something in what she sees makes her anxious. She sits still for a moment and suddenly blurts out without warning and in a disapproving tone of voice, "Look at the little copycat. Louise, stop that! Don't be such a copycat." By withholding approval the great-grandmother is demonstrating one of the principal ways in which learning is directed away from conscious imitation, which she obviously disapproves. Children, of course, are exceedingly sensitive to this process.

In order to serve humankind, learning, like sex, cannot run wild but has to be channeled and at times directed. There is much to learn of the details of how this process works in different cultures, and it is just barely possible that by studying others we Americans, who pride ourselves on our efficiency, might actually learn things that would help us to break out educational log jam. Our current approach to the teaching of reading is just one of the many obvious defects in American pedagogy. It is a symptom that something is wrong with our way of teaching. Instead of being rewarding for the child, learning has often become painful and difficult.

On Truk, the atoll in the Southwest Pacific, children

are permitted to reach the age of nine or ten before anyone begins to get technical with them about what they are supposed to know. As the Trukese phrase it, "He doesn't know yet, he is only a child." Americans tend to correct children rather impatiently. With us, learning is supposed to be endowed with a certain amount of pressure so that the fast learner is valued over the one who learns slowly. Some cultures seem to place less emphasis on speed and perhaps a little more on learning correctly. On the other hand, the current educational mode in the United States is to tell the child to guess if he doesn't know the meaning of a word. Not the best training for future scientists.

Americans like to think that children must "understand" what they have learned. What happens, of course, is that a good deal of material that would be simple enough to acquire without frills is made more difficult by the complex, and often erroneous, explanations that go with it. Somehow the fetish of explanation and logic as a process does not seem to weigh down the Arab or the Japanese, yet both have made singular contributions to the world of science.

How people learn to learn differently will continue to be an area of investigation for some time to come. As it now stands, however, these differences represent one of the barriers that have to be overcome each time two people raised in different cultures interact over any but the shortest period of time. The American will say, "Why can't the South Americans learn to be on time?" or "Why can't the Thai learn to boil the water for the ice cubes?" The answer, of course, is because no one taught them in a way which was consistent with how they learned everything else in life.

8. *Play*. In the course of evolution, play has been a relatively recent and not too well understood addition to living processes. It is well developed in mammals but not

so easily recognizable in birds, and its role as an adaptive mechanism is yet to be pinned down. However, one can say that it is interwoven into all of the other PMS. People laugh and tell jokes, and if you can learn the humor of a people and really control it you know that you are also in control of nearly everything else. Many peoples around the world have what are known as "joking relationships," and even in our own culture there is a category of relationship known as the "playmate." There are *places* and *times* for play—such as recreation rooms in houses and recreation areas in parks—as well as a vast amusement industry which keeps flourishing. Play and learning are intimately intertwined, and it is not too difficult to demonstrate a relationship between intelligence and play. Some games like chess and Chinese checkers are almost entirely a function of a specific type of intellectual development.

Play and the PMS of defense are also closely related; humor is often used to protect or hide vulnerabilities. Another example of the close relationship between play and defense is the practice exercises and maneuvers of the military which are spoken of as "war games."

One of the cardinal features of much western European play is that often it involves competition. As a consequence, games among the Pueblo of New Mexico, even races, seem very strange to us because they may involve an old man and a little boy in the same race with young men. The function of the race is not to beat someone else but only to "do one's very best." In fact, play with us is seldom an autonomous activity. In the Old West, to take an extreme example, there are often a certain amount of violence associated with play—jokes had an earthy flavor and often hurt or embarrassed the butt of the joke. In general, American humor is a binary type of humor, which is either turned on or off. In the Far East, however, one encounters a continuum, a wide spectrum of subtle degrees of enjoyment.

9. *Defense.* For humans and animals alike, defense is a specialized activity of tremendous importance. The ethologist studying lower life forms has traditionally examined and described the defensive mechanisms of the organisms studied. The ethologist may be familiar with these even before uncovering such basic processes as the details of an animal's diet. The opossum plays dead, the lizard changes the color of its coat to match the surrounding background, the turtle draws into its shell, the skunk deploys its odors and the squid its cloud of ink, birds travel in flocks to confuse hawks. These are only a few of the defensive devices that can be named by any schoolchild.

Human beings have elaborated their defensive techniques with astounding ingenuity not only in warfare, but also in religion, medicine, and law enforcement. They must defend themselves not only against potentially hostile forces in nature but against those within human society. They also must cope with the destructive forces within their own persons. Religion is concerned with warding off both the dangers in nature and within the individual. Law-enforcement agencies have been developed to deal with offenders against society, and armies are used against other societies. Medicine, too, defends the welfare of the groups as well as the individual against disease.

Since the functions of religion have been more completely documented and are more widely understood in the cross-cultural sense than those of medicine, law enforcement, or warfare, it will be treated only briefly. There is, however, one main point which should be kept in mind about the way different cultures tend to treat religion. With the possible exception of the people of the U.S.S.R., Americans have tended to compartmentalize religion and to reduce its social function more than any other people. The Navajo regard many activities, such as medicine, entertainment, sports, and science, as religious activities. In the Middle East, Islam plays a more pervasive role than Christianity does today in Europe. People in the Western world have difficulty grasping the extent to which religion infiltrates all aspects of life in the Arab world. The content of religion, its organization, and the manner in which it is integrated with the rest of life varies greatly from culture to culture.

Medicine varies too as one moves about the globe. Though Western medicine has achieved remarkable successes, we should not close our minds to the possibilities that other systems of healing can prevent untold suffering. Scholars have accumulated extensive material on the curing practices of other societies. The voodoo of Haiti, medicine men of the Navajo, and the herb doctor of the Chinese are well known to almost everyone. Like religion, medical practices are rigidly adhered to and given up only after everything else has failed. Basic attitudes toward sickness also differ. As Margaret Mead once pointed out, Americans have the underlying feeling that if they are sick, they are being bad. The Navajo, in turn, rarely blame themselves; they feel that if they are sick, they may have inadvertently stepped on a place that was taboo or that a bad person has bewitched them.

Like medicine, which is a defense against the ravages of disease, warfare which humans use against enemies, is also held in the tight vise of culture. In many ways it is as ritualistic as religion in its formal patterns. A striking example of this occurred during World War II. Since the Japanese cultural system ignored the contingency that Japanese troops might be taken alive, it provided no instruction for its soldiers as to how they should behave as prisoners. The result was that most POWs had no sense of military security, freely responded to interrogation, and cooperated with their captors to a degree which Europeans consider traitorous. In Korea, the American military assumed that U.S. prisoners would act properly even without specific training on how to behave under the stress of capture. Reports from the Korean War on the behavior of American men who were taken prisoner indicate that Americans are quite vulnerable psychologically. The simple rule of "tell 'em your name, rank, and serial number, nothing else," didn't work. Many Americans talked too much. Needless numbers died, many defected or were killed, and none escaped. The main reason was that they were operating according to one culture pattern and were unprepared to cope with either the North Korean or Chinese Communist pattern. Most had been led to believe that they would be treated very badly by the Communists and were thrown off base when they occasionally got "soft" treatment. Small kindnesses by Communists became magnified because of the physical hardship of prison life. Some Americans assumed that because they were prisoners the war was over for them and that they were no longer under military control. The cultural glue which held their life together crumbled under the pressure which the Communists applied so artfully. On their part, the Communists were miscued by the American pattern of egalitarianism, the lack of clear-cut class boundaries, and the fact that American leadership has to emerge informally for each new situation. When the Communists saw American prisoners going to one man with their problems or to get advice, they would suspect a conspiracy. The Communists would then remove this potential leader of the group and send him away. As a result, group support, sanctions, and controls failed to develop. The Turks fighting in Korea fared much better. They simply told the Communists who their leader was and made it clear that, in the event of his removal, the next in line would be leader, and so on down to the lowliest private. This meant that there was always a replacement for any leader the Communists removed. The Turk organization remained intact.

10. *Exploitation.* In order to exploit the environment all organisms adapt their bodies to meet specialized environmental conditions. A few examples: the long neck of the giraffe (adapted to high foliage of trees), the teeth of the saber-toothed tiger, toes of the tree sloth, hoof of the horse, and for humans, the opposable thumb. Occasionally organisms have developed specialized extensions of their bodies to take the place of what the body itself might do and thereby free the body for other things. Among these ingenious natural developments are the web of the spider, cocoons, nests of birds and fish. When humans appeared with their specialized bodies, such extention activities came into their own as a means of exploiting the environment.

Today our species has developed extensions for practically everything we used to do with our bodies. The evolution of weapons begins with the teeth and the fist and ends with the atom bomb. Clothes and houses are extensions of our biological temperature-control mechanisms. Furniture takes the place of squatting and sitting on the ground. Power tools, glasses, TV, telephones, and books which carry the voice across both time and space are examples of material extensions. Money is a way of extending and storing labor. Our transportation networks now do what we used to do with our feet and backs. In fact, all man-made material things can be treated as extensions of what was once done with the body or some specialized part of the body.

Materials and the rest of culture are intimately entwined. People sometimes mistake material elaboration or its absence for the whole of culture, but, in fact, each Primary Message System (PMS) has a material aspect which is closely associated with it. Men and women dress differently, tools go with work, time and space are measured with instruments, there are toys for play, books for learning, and even material signs of status. The relationship between materials and language is particularly close. Not only does each material thing have a name, but language and materials are often handled in much the same way. It is impossible to think of culture without language or materials. Think how difficult it would be to teach someone how to make a stone ax without being able to talk at all. At least you would need to be able to communicate something that stands for "No, not this way, that way."

One reason for stressing the relationship between language and materials is that there has been considerable discussion among anthropologists as to when language first came into being. It is generally accepted that it started a long time ago, but it is difficult to say just how long ago. My own estimate would be that, because of the intimate relationship between language and material culture, verbal communication arose at the same time as tool-making, sometime between 500,000 and 2,000,000 years ago. Philip Lieberman's definitive work on the biology and evolution of language places this date at 250,000 years ago when *Homosapiens* emerged and true culture began. The time between 2,000,000 years and 250,000 years ago can be considered as the proto-cultural period—a transition period between pre-culture and culture.

The close relationship between language and materials finds parallels in the linkage between other Primary Message Systems. For example, association and defense are functions of each other (people form "protective associations," etc.), as are work and play, bisexuality and learning, and space and time. Of this group only the relation between bisexuality and learning may seem obscure, and then only to a member of our own culture.

Those who belong to other societies may make this connection immediately. In our own culture the dividing line between the sexes has become fuzzy, but it is still true, even in the United States, that the variant of the culture which we acquire while growing up is largely a function of one's sex. If this were not true, there would be little cultural difference between the sexes.

By the way of summary, it is important to remember that culture is not one thing but a complex series of activities interrelated in many ways, activities with origins deeply buried in a past when there were no cultures and no humans. The development of language and technology, an interrelated pair, made possible the storing of knowledge. It gave us a lever to pry out the secrets of nature. It was the necessary condition for that burst of creativeness which we think of as culture in the highest sense. Well-developed langauge and technology are somehow closely associated with our present form, although just how this came about is not clearly understood. None of this would have been possible if it had not been for the highly evolved infra-cultural systems elaborated by lower organisms. By the time humans came along much of the evolution basic to culture had taken place in the very systems that are thought of as most characteristically human.

Each PMS is obviously so rich and complex that it can be made the subject of a lifetime's work. It is embarrassing to deal with such broad and inclusive fields in such a summary manner, but to skip over them would be to deprive the reader of a sense of how densely intricate the origins of culture are. The last generalization that should be made about culture is that it not only has great breadth and depth in the historical sense but that it also has other dimensions of equal importance. Culture is saturated with both emotion and intelligence. Many things that humans do in the acquired realm are not even experienced, for they are accomplished out-of-awareness. But a great part of human activity is either the direct result of conscious thought or suffused with emotion and feeling. The way behavior—and culture—can be divided by the degree of awareness or feeling which attaches to it is the subject of the chapters which follow.

4

THE MAJOR
TRIAD

One of the most dramatic and revolutionary of Freud's achievements was his elaborate analysis of the role of the unconscious. Those who are familiar with his writings will recall how much time he spent trying to convince people that such events as a slip of the lip or pen, as well as dreams, were all evidence of hidden forces in humans over which they exercise no conscious control. This revelation of an unconscious world led to further psychological explorations which introduced a new dimension into human behavior. No longer were we considered to be entirely rational, ruled by logic. No longer could we be conceived of as an elegantly tooled machine run from the higher centers of the brain. We became much less predictable but much more interesting when viewed as a battleground of conflicting drives and emotions, many of them hidden. After Freud it became common to think of ourselves as beings who existed on a number of different levels at once.

Freud also relied heavily on the communicative significance of our acts rather than our words. Freud distrusted the spoken word, and a good deal of his thinking was based on the assumption that words hid much more than they revealed. He depended more on communication in the larger context, on the symbols of dreams and the meaning of insignificant events which would ordinarily go unnoticed and were therefore not subject to the censors that we all have within us. Despite his massive discoveries, what Freud really lacked was a theory of communication. Today, years after the major part of his theory was laid down, psychoanalysis still lacks a systematic way of describing the events of communication which occur between doctor and patient.

Revolutionary as Freud's conception of the unconscious was, his view that it is inaccessible to direct examination was a stumbling block to further systematic analysis. Among those who did not agree with the Freudian scheme was the late Washington psychiatrist, Harry Stack Sullivan. Sullivan regarded the unconscious as the dissociated facets of the personality that are out of the person's awareness. His formulations were of great value to the social scientist because they cleared the way for further research. Sullivan taught that each of us has an *ideal* self, which we approve, and other selves which we may not find so attractive. Some of these are so repugnant to us that only the very strong can tolerate them. Therefore, the workaday, actual, operating self is seen as a composite of behavior patterns which Sullivan called dynamisms. The dynamisms are ways of integrating with other human beings. A person is aware of some of them, while others are dissociated and therefore hidden to the individual but revealed to the world. This notion that there are significant portions of the personality that exist out of one's own awareness but which are there for everyone else to see may seem frightening. The point, however, is a crucial one and will grow in importance as people begin to grasp its implications. What Sullivan said, in effect, was that the unconscious is not hidden to anyone except the individual who hides those parts which persons significant in his or her early life have disapproved. While they are dissociated or hidden from himself, they are there for trained observers to see and they can therefore be analyzed.

Sullivan's contribution was a great one. It helped to dispel a good deal of psychoanalytic mumbo jumbo, opening up wide horizons for research into the interpersonal process.

Both Freud and Sullivan drew heavily on the works of anthropologists—Freud indirectly, using anthropology to support his views, Sullivan in a more immediate way. Sullivan worked actively with the greatest descriptive linguist of our time, Edward Sapir, the man who laid the foundations for modern descriptive linguistics. While the psychologists were looking to anthropology to learn more about humans as social beings, the anthropologists were using the theories of psychoanalysis in their attempts to formulate more satisfying theories of culture. One of the most significant of these borrowed theories was that culture existed on two levels: *overt* culture, which is visible and easily described, and *covert* culture, which is not visible and presents difficulties even to the trained observer. The iceberg analogy was commonly used when teaching this theory to students and laymen alike. When it soon turned out that this theory was inadequate to describe the cultural picture, anthropologists like Kluckhohn started speaking of *explicit* and *implicit* culture. Explicit culture, such things as law, was what people talk about and can be specific about. Implicit culture, such as feelings about success, was what they took for granted or what existed on the fringes of awareness.

Much has been written about the implicit assumptions of various cultures, including our own. This approach is a good one and has been responsible for a number of valuable insights. However, the level of abstraction in the implicit-explicit culture concept is so high that it is impossible to build on it easily. The discovery that one of the implicit assumptions of American life is that hard work will be rewarded may explain a good deal about behavior in this country, but it is difficult to combine with other similar insights to form a broader generalization of American life. Like many other abstractions about culture, this one leaves us with the feeling, "Where do we go from here?" Despite its level of abstraction, the view that culture comprises some aspects that can be talked about and some that cannot remains valuable. It also provides another example of how we have come to see behavior on two levels.

Freud distinguished between conscious and unconscious; Sullivan between the in-awareness and out-of-awareness. Anthropologists like the late Ralph Linton spoke of overt and covert culture; others used terms like implicit and explicit, which were applied to the assumptions underlying behavior as well as the patterns controlling it. This bipolar way of analyzing events soon spread to other fields, such as political science and scientific management. Both disciplines adopted the terms formal and informal when describing behavior patterns, management procedures, and organizational structure. The use of these polarized categories made it possible to make distinctions which were important and which had not been made before. Moreover, they were consistent with the American tendency to see things as opposites—in black and white. The ease with which Americans tend to polarize their thoughts about events may make it difficult for them to embrace an approach which employs three categories rather than two. Yet that is what I would like to propose here: a theory which suggests that culture has three levels. I have termed these the formal, informal, and technical, familiar terms but with new and expanded meanings.

Trager and I arrived at this tripartite theory as a result of some rather detailed and lengthy observations as to the way in which Americans use, talk about and handle time. Our observations revealed that instead of two kinds of time there were actually three kinds of time: formal time, which everyone knows about and takes for granted and which is well worked into daily life; informal time, which has to do with situational or imprecise references like "awhile," "later," "in a minute," and so on; technical time, an entirely different system used by scientists and technicians, in which even the terminology may be unfamiliar to the nonspecialist. Having observed how these time systems are used and learned, and knowing something of their history, we were able to demonstrate that in other areas of life we are also bound by the formal, informal and technical paradigm. In other words, we discovered that people have not two but three modes of behavior. Our generalizations about time had much broader applications than we originally supposed.

The sport of skiing offers an excellent example of the formal, informal, and technical modes. Some years ago in the town of Grand Lake, Colorado, on the snowy western slope of the Rockies, there was a tradition that everyone had to use skis to get around in the wintertime. New schoolteachers transferred into the area had to learn to ski, and even the school principal and the school band were on skis. Small children acquired the basic of skiing soon after they could walk. When one watched these people move about it was as though the skis were an actual extension of the foot, a highly adapted organ for locomotion. Each person had developed his or her own highly individualistic style, just as everyone has his or her own way of walking. When skiing competitions took place some of the villagers were better than others, while many did not compete at all. The main thing was that everyone skied. No one questioned the fact that this was desirable. Skiing was taken for granted as a part of the daily life of the town; it was, to use the term which will reappear in these pages again and again, a *formal* tradition.

At the same time, there were a few hardy souls in Denver and other nearby towns who used to take to skis for pleasure, as a part-time activity. There was no pressure on these persons to ski. They simply liked to get out in the open. Some of them had real talent; others weren't so skilled. This group skied because it enjoyed the fun and the exercise and the beautiful scenery of the mountains and the camaraderie of the sport. They were not highly conscious of how they skied, what technique they used, or how the skill could be taught. They would say, "Watch me," or "Do it like this," and that was about as far as they could go. I never will forget the time when one of my friends who had been watching this weekly trek to the mountains finally decided to come along. He was an excellent athlete who had once been a Golden Gloves champion, so he had no lack of natural co-ordination and control. However, when he first put on skis the result was comic and disastrous at once. As soon as he tried to take a step, down he went. Encumbered by his skis, he could barely get up. The newcomer was beset by all sorts of problems which demanded skilled and technical analysis if they were to be solved quickly. Unfortunately the best that these Sunday skiers could manage was something like this: "You bend your knees and take off. Eventually you'll get the hang of it." Their conception of skiing was *informal*, a view which is no better expressed than in the phrase, "You'll get the hang of it."

At the same time that the townspeople on the western slope were acquiring skiing and the informal skiers from Denver were making their weekly pilgrimage to the mountains, thousands of feet of film were being taken in the Alps of wonderfully skilled skiers rushing down slopes, turning, climbing, and coming to a stop. These films were analyzed, and the whole process was broken down into its components or isolates, as they can be called. In addition to the components, broader patterns were also analyzed. After a while it was decided that skiing was not an art which had to be restricted to the gifted. Anyone with patience and a modicum of control could be taught to ski, since the components had been so well identified that they could be talked about and described *technically*. Moreover, the uniformity of skill that could be achieved by these new technically trained skiers was so amazing that it made possible the later tremendous popularity of the sport. Few people like to fail in what they do, and with the new methods of teaching, a few hours instruction could give enough skill and confidence so that a newcomer could still have fun.

In the light of our previous hypothesis that all cultural behavior is biologically based, it might be assumed that the formal, informal, and technical aspects of life are also rooted in man's physiological organism. Unfortunately, however, the subtle chain of connections between the physiology of the nervous system and human behavior still remains a comparative mystery. At present the most we can say is that one would expect to find that these three types of behavior spring from three different parts of the nervous system. This assumption can be inferred from a characteristic of behavior which everyone has experienced: It is extremely difficult to practice more than one element of the formal, informal, technical triad at the same time without paralyzing results. People who type as an informal activity know that if they start thinking in detail technically about what they are doing with their fingers and where the letters are located they will have trouble. Beginners who are studying shorthand are told that they "have to get it in their fingers" or they will not pick up any speed. A friend of mine, a neuropsychiatrist, once pointed out that it was enough to draw attention to one level of activity while a person was operating on another to stop all coherent thought. He used the example of a mother who is mad at her son and is berating him. The boy looks up and says, "Gee, Mommy, your mouth moves funny when you're mad." The mother is apt to become speechless. MacLean's work on our *triune* brain has since supported this hypothesis.

One more generalization that should be kept in mind about formal, informal, and technical integrations is that while one will dominate, all three are present in any given situation. To refer back to the skiers for a moment, it is easy to see that even those who approach skiing as a formal activity will have to get mildly technical about it, otherwise they would have difficulty talking about the details of skiing. Everyone has his or her own style (the informal), but the informal has the formal as a base. If one were to compare the three groups of skiers, one would find that the formal mountain skiers and the informal skiers from the plains had much more in common with each other than either of them had with the European technical skiers. The technical, of course, very quickly develops its own new formal systems. Science, for example, which we think of as being the very essence of the technical, actually has built up within it a large number of formal systmes that nobody questions. These have to do with the methodology of science, the insistence on the objectivity of the members of the scientific community, their honesty in regard to their own work and the work of others. As a matter of fact, a good deal of what goes under the heading of science would more appropriately be classed as a new formal system which is very rapidly displacing or altering our older formal systems centered in folk beliefs and religion.

Most medicine as it is practiced, in contrast to medical

research, can be more appropriately classed as formal. This is not meant to be a criticism of doctors. If they did not develop formal systems their patients would force them into it. The so-called social sciences or behavioral sciences are shot through with procedural ritual that graduate students learn and later pass on to their own students. One zealous sociologist developed an index to reflect the degree to which a paper was "scientific." He devised a rating system derived from the relative proportion of text to footnotes and the quantity of statistics in relation to text!

FORMAL LEARNING

Formal activities are taught by precept and admonition. The adult mentor molds the young according to patterns she or he has never questioned. He or she will correct the child saying, "Boys don't do that," or "You can't do that," using a tone of voice indicating that what you are doing is unthinkable. There is no question in the mind of the speaker about where he/she stands and where every other adult stands. In correcting their children's speech, parents will say, "Not 'goed'! Went!" The burden of this communication is that no other form is conceivably acceptable. Formal patterns are almost always learned when a mistake is made and someone corrects it. Technical learning also begins with mistakes and corrections, but it is done with a different tone of voice and the student is offered reasons for the correction. An error made by many parents and teachers these days is to try to explain formal behavior in the same way one goes about outlining the reasons for technical behavior. This is a signal to the child that there is an alternative, that one form is as good as another! A great mistake. The details of formal learning are *binary*, of a yes-no, right-wrong character. You either break a taboo or you don't, you steal your neighbor's coconut or you don't, you say "boyses" for boys or you don't. Hundreds of little details add up until they amount to a formal system which nobody questions.

INFORMAL LEARNING

Informal learning is of an entirely different character from either the technical or the formal. The principal agent is a *model* used for imitation. Whole clusters of related activities are learned at a time, in many cases without the knowledge that they are being learned at all or that there are patterns or rules governing them. A child may be puzzled about something and ask her or his mother for the rules. "You'll find out about that later, dear," or "Look around you and see what people are doing; use your eyes!" Whenever statements like the one that follows are made, on can be sure that the activity is an informal one: "Mother—how does a woman get a man to marry her?" "Well, it's a little hard to describe, but when you get bigger you'll find out. There's plenty of time for learning." The child is treated to this kind of remark so often that he/she automatically translates it as, "Don't ask questions, look around and see what people do." In the United States the most important area in which this type of learning operates is sex. For the most part, sex is learned informally—a fact which might account for the morbid fascination it exercises on people. When someone like the late Alfred Kinsey tried to systematize the available knowledge about sexual behavior he was commonly greeted with the question, "How do you know? Were you there?"

Hollywood is famous for hiring various experts to teach people technically what most people learn informally. A case in point is the story about the children of one movie couple who noticed a new child in the neighborhood climbing a tree. The children immediately wanted to be given the name of his instructor in tree climbing.

Entire systems of behavior made up of hundreds of thosands of details are passed from generation to generation, and nobody can give the rules for what is happening. Only when these rules are broken do we realize they exist. For example, the writer used to ask his audience of people going abroad to give the rule for *first naming* in the United States. They could give a few, in vague terms, but pretty soon they would be floundering. In the end they would remark, "You know, when you look at it that way it's pretty hard to pin these things down."

Unconsciously a great many people recognize the validity of using models as the major instrument of informal learning. As a whole, women in the United States are more aware of this than men, though they too are apt to overlook imitation for what it is—a way of acquiring appropriate behavior—a way of becoming a member of society. Everyone has seen small boys mimic their father's walk or imitate a TV hero or, at the worst, mimic some unsavory character who hangs out at the corner drugstore. In many cases the mother does not approve of Junior's selection of models, though she may not even be aware of her reasons. By disapproving strongly, she may make a hash of the informal learning propensities of her children by interfering with their early attempts at imitation.

TECHNICAL LEARNING

Technical learning, in its pure form, is close to being a one-way street. It is usually transmitted in explicit terms from the teacher to the student, either orally or in writing. Often it is preceded by a logical analysis and proceeds in coherent outline form. Some of the best examples of technical teaching can be found in the armed services, where techniques have been worked out for handling large masses of recruits. This success is further confirmation of the point that technical learning is an inevitable concomitant of teaching large numbers of people. Unlike informal learning, it depends less on the aptitude of the student and the selection of adequate models, but more on the intelligence with which the material is analyzed and presented.

During World War II, when great numbers of trained technicians were in demand, it was assumed that those who had mechanical aptitude would make good airplane mechanics. A careful analysis of this assumption proved otherwise. It turned out that a good shoe clerk in civilian life would become a better mechanic for military purposes than someone who had fixed cars most of his life and learned on a Model-T Ford. The critical trait was not mechanical aptitude but the ability of the trainee to follow instructions. The Army then worked out its instruction manuals so meticulously that the best recruit turned out to be a mildly obsessional person who could read and follow directions. The last thing they wanted was someone with his own ideas on how to fix equipment.

To recapitulate briefly: The formal is a two-way process. The learner tries, makes a mistake, is corrected ("No, not the right side of the horse, the left side! Remember, never approach a horse from the right!"). Formal learning tends to be suffused with emotion. Informal learning is largely a matter of the learner picking others as models. Sometimes this is done deliberately, but most commonly it occurs out-of-awareness. In most cases the model does not take part in this process except as an object of imitation. Technical learning moves in the other direction. The knowledge rests with the teacher's skill which is a function of his or her knowledge and analytic ability. If the analysis is sufficiently clear and thorough, the teacher doesn't even have to be there. She or he can write it down or put it on a record. In real life one finds a little of all three in almost any learning situation. One type, however, will always dominate.

FORMAL AWARENESS

Compared to many other societies, our does not invest *tradition* with an enormous weight. Even our most powerful traditions do not generate the binding force which is common in some other cultures. For example, the Zuñi of New Mexico have a predominantly formal culture that exerts a heavy pressure on its members. People simply cannot disregard social pressures and remain in the pueblo. If they want to leave and live with strangers the rest of their lives, they can fly in the face of tradition, otherwise they have to conform. We Americans have emphasized the informal at the expense of the formal. There are, however, pockets, like old New England and certain parts of the South, where tradition plays a vital role in life. This style of life in which formal awareness predominates has been elegantly sketched in novels like J. P. Marquand's *The Late George Apley*. Formal awareness is an approach to life that asks with surprise: "Is there any other way?" Formally aware people are more likely to be influenced by the past than they are by the present or future. Formal awareness is awareness of what Apley would call "what's right, what ought to be there."

INFORMAL AWARENESS

The term informal awareness is paradoxical because it describes a situation in which much of what goes on exists almost entirely *out-of-awareness*. Nothing, however, is hidden in any sense of the word. In fact, it is doubtful if there is any part of culture which is really hidden once we know how to go about looking for the eloquent signs.

In informal activity the absence of awareness permits a high degree of patterning. A moment's reflection will show that in walking or in driving a car awareness of the process is apt to be an impediment to smooth performance; similarly, too much awareness of the process of writing or speaking can get in the way of what one is trying to say. The informal is therefore made up of activities or mannerisms which we once learned but which are so much a part of our everyday life that they are done automatically. They are, in fact, often blocked when cerebration takes place.

All this has been known in one way or another for a long time, but no one has understood the degree to which informal activities permeate life nor how the out-of-awareness character of informal acts often leads to untold difficulty in a cross-cultural situation. The tone of voice of the upper-class English which sounds so affected to many Americans is an example of just this kind of activity which, unless properly understood, can be a stumbling block between individuals from different cultures.

What I have described is not to be confused with neuroses in which certain aspects of the personality are also out-of-awareness. The psychological literature is filled with references to dissociated behavior, unconscious behavior, and so on, but these are deviations from the norm and should not be confused with the informal.

TECHNICAL AWARENESS

While all technical behavior has in it some of the formal as well as the informal, it is characterized by the fact that it is fully conscious behavior. Its very explicitness and the fact that it can be written down and recorded and even taught at a distance differentiates it from the other two types of integration. The very essence of the

technical is that it is on the highest level of consciousness. Science is largely technical.

FORMAL AFFECT

Affect is a technical term used by psychologists to
describe feelings as distinct from thought. The nontech-
nical reader may prefer to substitute "emotion" or "feeling"
whenever the term "affect" is used. Whenever violations
of formal norms occur, they are accompanied by a tide
of emotion. One can get an idea of how people feel
about formal systems by thinking of a person who has
been supported all his or her life by a very strong prop.
Remove the prop and you shake the foundations of life.
Deep emotions are associated with the formal in almost
every instance.

Part of the success of the late Clarence Darrow was
attributable to his being a past master at invoking formal
systems to sway juries. Darrow was and remains a contro-
versial figure. Many people used to look upon him as a
scoundrel who succeeded in having thieves and murderers
acquitted when they should have been sent to jail. Today
he is still a figure of great popular interest, but those who
write about him tend to see him in a new way. They
emphasize his humanity rather than his superb command
of the law. For the law is technical and dry and supposedly blind to human emotions—a cardinal sin in this age.
Darrow dressed in an old sloppy suit. He appealed to the
common man—people could identify with him. He was
their type, the country bumpkin who outsmarts the city
slicker. Now it is obvious that in addition to knowing his
law well he also knew his culture. He realized that most
people do not understand the law but will stand up for
their own formal systems and even weep over them when
they see them outraged. This was Darrow's strength, and
the only time he really failed to capitalize on it was when

he was called to Honolulu for the Massie case in 1932. There he faced a jury made up of members who had different formal systems. The Chinese jurors weren't a bit moved by his strategies rooted in *haole* culture.

In time, as formal systems become firmer they become so identified with the process of nature itself that alternative ways of behavior are thought of as unnatural—if not impossible. Yet this rigidity has its advantages. People who live and die in formal cultures tend to take a more relaxed view of life than the rest of us because the boundaries of behavior are so clearly marked, even to the permissible deviations. There is never any doubt in anybody's mind that, as long as one adheres to the norms, one knows what to expect from others. Those who are familiar with the difference between Catholicism in Latin America, where the population is so predominantly Catholic that religion is not an issue, and in the United States, where we are more technical about religion, have an excellent example of how people live under the same institution of religion yet react differently, depending upon whether it is administered formally, informally or technically.

INFORMAL AFFECT

There is little or no affect attached to informal behavior as long as things are going along nicely according to the unwritten or unstated rules. Anxiety, however, follows quickly when this tacit etiquette is breached. Extreme discomfort is apt to occur when someone stands too close or uses a first name prematurely. What happens next depends upon the alternatives provided by the culture for handling anxiety. Ours includes withdrawal and anger. In Japan men giggle or laugh nervously. The alternative responses are comparatively restricted and automatic. The leeway for emotional response in the informal is much less than one might expect. The point is that the emotions associated with deviation from informal norms are themselves acquired informally and are limited by the fact that people do not realize that their response is learned or that there is any other way to respond. A comparable situation exists in language: In English, one of the most common ways of indicating that one is asking a question is by ending with a rising inflection. That there might be other inflections which achieve the same purpose simply does not occur to one. In this sort of thing it seems "natural" that the repertoire would be somewhat limited.

TECHNICAL AFFECT

The technical is characterized by a suppression of feelings, since they tend to interfere with effective functioning. One of the great differences between the real professional and the amateur boxer is that the amateur is likely to become really angry, whereas the professional prides himself in keeping his wits about him and his temper in control. The scientist's approach to his or her work is so well known that we need say little about it. In general the technical person becomes emotionally involved only when the technical rules of the game are not followed. Once a technical foundation is laid down, it seems to be important to adhere to it.

Because it is so explicit, the technical in our society has become associated with authority and law and other structures which embody uncompromising attitudes. A mother who is provoked by a child may find herself using the child's full name as she calls her or him to account. The child immediately knows that she/he has stepped out of line and Mother means business because she is getting technical. The formal and the technical are often confused. For one thing, the formal is supported by technical props. It is the technical that people often resort to when all else fails.

The whole matter of deviation from norms bristles with complexity. For example, children never know where the line is until they step across it. The manner in which they are reprimanded provides the glue that holds together these systems in later life. Children never know until they find out by trial and error whether they have violated a formal, informal, or technical norm. There are gross differences in regard to norms from one culture to another. Within the confines of a diverse culture such as our own, what is a formal matter at one time may become informal later, what is viewed technically by one group may be informal within the next. To return to children, it seems to be important that they know that there are norms and lines beyond which they cannot go despite the leeway allowed them. They also need to know that there are some norms that are comparatively unchangeable and which can be depended upon throughout life. From a theoretical point of view the relation of the formal, informal, and technical to norms becomes of great importance.

FORMAL ATTITUDES TOWARD CHANGE

Formal systems are characterized by a great tenacity, a trait which satisfies a deep need in all societies and individuals. Without this tenacious consistency in life, life itself would not be possible. Originally, with the early vertebrates, instinct or innate behavior patterns provided for this consistency. With the advent of acquisition as an additional adaptive mechanism the role of the instinct began to fade until in humans it plays a negligible role in life. It is formal culture that does a job closely analogous to instinct. Everybody can depend upon it almost as though it were instinctual. It is the base from

which the rest of culture springs and around which it is
built.

Except under special circumstances, the formal
changes slowly, almost imperceptibly. It is also highly
resistant to forced change from the outside—a point now
well known to many of our technicians working in foreign
countries. Since the formal is seldom recognized as such,
the American abroad often has the impression that other
people's formal systems are unnecessary, immoral, crazy,
backward, or a remnant of some outworn value that
America gave up some time ago. Afif Tannous, a Leba-
nese-American sociologist, tells of a case of the Arab
villagers who refused to let outsiders clean up a water
hole contaminated with typhoid and install a pump. The
reader may wonder what there was about having a nice
clean water supply that violated the formal norms of Arab
villagers. Strange as it seems to us, Arab villagers like the
water they drink. It has a nice strong taste which it gets
from the camels. Water with them is thought to be almost
sacred. If the men of a given village are strong or brave
or fertile or smart it is because of the water they drink.
In some parts of the Arab world it is considered sissy to
drink clean water. The villagers saw no relation between
disease and the water that made their men strong. Babies
died because God willed it, and who were they to go
tampering with the will of God? This story underlines
the necessity of understanding and accepting the formal
systems of other peoples first in order to work effectively
within them.

Alexander Leighton's book, *The Governing of Men*, also
provides a penetrating example of how a misunderstanding about formal systems of leadership stalled a government program with the Japanese internees during the
war. Once this was corrected, these same systems were
used quite successfully. The American mistake was to
select construction foremen according to their qualifica-

tions—a natural error, considering the great emphasis we put on technical competence. The Japanese, who had suffered insult, the loss of their possessions, and forcible imprisonment without losing their patience, finally went on strike when this happened. They were outraged that the Americans had completely disregarded the social hierarchy which figures so importantly in Japanese society. The solution to this problem lay in allowing the internees to choose their own leaders from among those who had the proper status. It mattered little that these honored old men spoke no English and knew less about engineering. They promptly picked young engineers as their advisers.

I am indebted to John Evans—son of Mabel Dodge Lujan and onetime superintendent of the Northern Pueblo Agency—who spent many years as a young man in Taos, for an exquisite example of a formal pattern. The Taos are an independent people who carefully guard their culture from the white man. They even make a secret of how to say "Thank you" in Taos. This makes it difficult for the governmental representatives whose job it is to work with them. According to Evans, there had been some difficulty finding an agricultural extension agent who could work with the Taos. Finally a young man was chosen who liked the Taos and who was careful to approach them slowly. Everything went along very well, and it seemed that he was, indeed, the right man for such a ticklish job. When spring arrived, however, Evans was visited in Albuquerque by the agriculturist, wearing a long face. Evans asked, "What's the matter? You look depressed." His visitor replied, "As a matter of fact, I am. I don't know what's wrong. The Indians don't like me any more. They won't do any of the things I tell them." Evans promised to find out what he could. The next time there was a council meeting at Taos he took one of the older Indians aside and asked him what was wrong between the tribe and the young man. His friend looked him in the eye and said, "John, he just doesn't know certain things! You know, John—*think*. . . ."

Suddenly Evans understood. In the spring the Taos believe that Mother Earth is pregnant. To protect the surface of the earth they do not drive their wagons to town, they take the shoes off their horses, they refuse to wear hard-soled shoes themselves. Our agriculturist had been trying to institute a program of early-spring plowing!

Often, however, the conflict between different formal systems in different cultures has a tragic outcome. During the Spanish conquest of the New World one of the reasons the Spaniards were able to take so much territory was that their formal systems were so radically different from the Indian system. The Spaniards fought to kill; the Aztecs fought to take prisoners. Like the Plains Indians to the north, the Aztecs were at a loss in dealing with an enemy who killed in battle. Because this was a formal system the Aztecs were not able to change it in time to save themselves or their society. Similarly, some American prisoners of war during World War II were not able to adapt to the deference patterns of their Japanese captors and thus save themselves needless torture. The Japanese formal view of life is that there must be order in the relations between men and that this order is expressed by people taking and demonstrating their positions in a hierarchy. People of higher status are addressed by certain polite forms; respect is shown by bowing quite low with the upper part of the body held rigid. The Americans who were captured by the Japanese felt it was a violation of their dignity to have to bow. The Japanese thought this showed extreme disrespect and threatened the very foundations of life.

The *formal* provides a broad pattern within whose outlines the individual actors can fill in the details for themselves. If they stay within the boundaries, life goes along smoothly. If not, they find themselves in trouble. For instance, if two men have a business appointment in the middle or late morning and one of them is five minutes late, there is no serious difficulty. A simple apology usually suffices. Though the formal system in our culture says that one must be punctual, it also provides for a certain amount of leeway. The norm can be violated in two principal ways: first, by going way beyond the permissible limit, so that it is obvious that you are deliberately flying in the face of custom; second, by ignoring the permissible informal leeway, becoming overly technical, and demanding an apology if someone is only twenty seconds late.

INFORMAL ATTITUDES TOWARD CHANGE

Mishandling the informal can often lead to serious difficulties which are apt to become aggravated since the participants in an informal situation are not fully conscious of what is going on. They only know that under a certain set of unstated rules they can act in a certain way and depend upon other people to react appropriately. This informal expectancy is often frustrated when there is a conflict between two patterns within the context of our own culture or in the more familiar case of a cross-cultural situation.

An example of a rather wearing cross-cultural conflict occurred in the West a number of years ago. Since no one was directly aware of what was going on, the result was a ludicrously tragic situation which persisted for some twenty years. The two cultures involved were the Spanish and the American; at the heart of the prolonged crisis was the differing view which each group takes of law, government, and family. The Latin-American Spanish have developed the institution of the family to a size, stability, and influence that are incredible to us. Their governments on the other hand do not occupy such an important position in the scheme of things as ours does. If something should happen or if something is wanted in a Latin-American country, families are apt to be better at handling the affair than the government. This informal tradition is associated with a different concept of law from our own. Law in Latin America is enforced technically (by the book), but it is mediated by family relationships. With us law courts, and particularly enforcement officers, are not supposed to be harsh and should be guided by the formal systems of the culture. That is, the law is never expected to be stricter than the rest of the culture. If it works undue hardships on people, then it has to be changed. When the American comes across a law which he/she considers to be unjust or which doesn't make sense, he or she is much more likely to violate it than if she or he considers it realistic and sensible.

The point at which the Spanish and American patterns collided in the western town was over the enforcement of the speed limit. For many years the town—predominantly Spanish in population and government—had a motorcycle policeman named Sancho, of Spanish cultural descent. His job was to enforce the speed limit of 15 mph which extended to the outskirts and included a stretch of two national highways. So assiduous was Sancho in his work that he was famous to all the townspeople as well as to the *americanos* who lived in the surrounding communities. Acting on the letter of the law, he would arrest people going 16 mph—an offense which was punishable by a fine of $12.75, a considerable sum of money during the depression years of the thirties.

The Spanish-Americans brought before the court usually had a cousin or an uncle sitting on the bench and were quickly acquitted. The *americanos*, who were rarely that lucky, became increasingly furious at the situation.

Finally they began plotting against Sancho. Once he was led out of town at 60 mph and then run off the road. His legs were so badly broken that he could no longer ride a motorcycle. When he emerged from the hospital he bought a fast roadster and went back to work. But from then on for the next ten or fifteen years life for Sancho became a series of "accidents." He no longer trusted anyone and arrested speeders with a drawn pistol. Even this did not prevent him from being severely beaten up from time to time by the anglos who resented being arrested for going 16 mph and who had to pay their fines. What the Americans did not understand—and for this they may easily be forgiven—is that the two cultures treat the same point of behavior quite differently and structure the informal into different parts of their respective systems. Technically, to the Spanish, the law was the law and 16 mph was an infraction of the law. Only after they were arrested did they invoke the informal by turning to that system of relatives which is equipped to deal with a weak government. Americans, on the other hand, allow themselves a certain amount of informal leeway in their interpretation of what constitutes a violation, but they tend to get *tough* (and technical) once the machinery of the law is set in motion. The idea of holding people precisely to 15 mph violates both our attitude toward laws (they should make sense) and our sense of informal leeway. Sancho's trouble was that he never had a model to show him how to deal with anglos.

On the whole, Americans have developed no system for making the law easy to live with, as have the Latin Americans. Our own formal system says that it is reprehensible to use influence and doubly so for public officials to show favoritism. We allow very little leeway here, on the grounds that unless a person is either foolish or guilty he or she would not have run afoul of the law in the first place. Laws may be broken in the United States, but there is a great reluctance to tamper with the legal machinery once it has got under way. As products of American culture we tend to have a difficult time overseas when the laws lack informal leeway in their enforcement. We see no alternative ways of making them livable. We find it hard to discover those points where there is leeway and, when we do, we are hesitant in using what we find out because it violates our own formal systems. What Americans really like and usually hold out for is for others to change their systems so that it "makes sense" like ours does.

There is, of course, a little of the informal in everything. What is confusing to people who travel or work overseas is that there is no way of knowing just where the leeway has been built into a situation. To make this doubly difficult, the local nationals can't describe the rules either. Furthermore, a formal system with very little give in it one time may show a great deal of flexibility a few years later. Arab attitudes toward women, for example, are changing very rapidly. What was constant for centuries no longer holds.

TECHNICAL ATTITUDES TOWARD CHANGE

When American technicians are prepared to work abroad, they must be warned to avoid introducing changes that violate formal norms. The technician may ask: "In what area, then, can I try to help these people help themselves and still not run afoul of the formal and the informal? Where can I have some real control over what goes on?" The answer, of course, is in the technical. Here one can introduce changes with the greatest ease without violating the norms of the other two systems. Just as the United States suffers no disruption in the course of constant progress in such things as the design of automobile engines, fuels, oil and metals, antibiotics and medicine, so comparable changes can be made in countries that have not progressed as far as we have technologically. Whatever changes are introduced have to be made in those parts of the lives of the local people *that are treated technically* or else they must be offered *as entirely new systems complete in themselves.* In many parts of Latin America, for example, air travel was introduced before the stage of the cart and the automobile had even been reached. It was easier to build airports than a road network. The same leapfrogging technology is being applied in Africa.

Usually, however, technical changes are small changes which have to do with the details of an operation. You can change the bore and stroke of a motor without changing the over-all design. You can alter the pitch of a propeller to conform to special conditions, change the construction material for a house without violating the formal norms that dictate the over-all design, put a steel point on a wooden plow without violating formal norms, make insectides in powder or liquid form to conform to local custom. By changing the emphasis from one of "making the soil more productive" to "feeding" the soil with fertilizer, modern agriculture can be made more acceptable the Indonesians, who, because of their formal religious beliefs, try to avoid controlling nature.

One of the most remarkable changes that have come to light in recent years is the one described by Margaret Mead in her report about the unique people of Manus in the South Pacific. The Manus Islanders treat their culture technically. They apparently have done so for such a long time that there is little evidence that they could accept any other attitude without seriously disrupting their lives. They experiment with their culture consciously, taking it apart and putting it together again to see how it works in different ways. With these propensities it was inevitable that close contact with Americans during the war would make available new systems of behavior and new ways of organizing society. This is what happened. The Manus apparently did the incredible thing of sitting down and saying to themselves, "Now let's organize a new society that's more in keeping with the outside world." They didn't wait for change to overtake them gradually, or drift off in small numbers and lose themselves among the whites. They sat down and designed a society from the ground up. What is not clear, of course, in view of the technical attitude toward life, is *where the formal core is* and what form it takes on Manus. One view that can be taken of what happened on Manus is that the things that were changed represented a relatively superficial fringe around a more stable and persisting core, just as the Pueblo potter may make variations in the designs she uses on the pot but is not likely to change the method of building up the walls, polishing, or firing.

Maria, a famous New Mexico potter, provides us with an excellent example of how small changes occur and how far-reaching their effects can be. She practices an art borrowed indirectly from Mexico and carried on by Pueblo women for some thirteen to fifteen hundred years.

The Pueblo women have always been notoriously conservative in their pottery making. Since slightly before the time of World War I their pottery began to deteriorate noticeably, a sign that Pueblo life was losing some of its integrative powers. As the indians moved farther and farther down the socio-economic scale in comparison to the whites, they began to lose self-respect. No one knows what would have happened if it had not been for three key figures: Maria and her husband Julian, both skilled craftsmen, and Kenneth Chapman, an anthropologist who saw what was happening and dedicated himself to reviving Pueblo crafts. Julian helped Maria with the pottery by occasionally painting the designs for her. This was one of those small technical changes that leads to bigger things. Maria was the best potter in San Ildefonso. The care and attention to detail in her work were obvious even to those who were not experts. By Pueblo standards she was an individualist. Unlike many of the others, her work did not deteriorate and therefore became even more popular. Chapman selected her work for promotion in the white world.

Once by accident two of Maria's pots turned black instead of red. A plain black pot that is not well made is hideous. A plain black pot that is beautifully made actually enables one to appreciate both the simplicity of the black as well as the expertness of the technique. Despite this, the San Ildefonso people had no place in their world for a plain black pot. The whites, on the other hand, had no tradition in regard to pottery, no preconception that it should be white or black or red. They thought it should be well made, smooth, and symmetrical. Once when Julian and Maria ran out of the red pottery they sold through a Santa Fe storekeeper, they gave him the two black "spoiled" pots. Before the man could get them back to his store he had sold them.

It was very easy for the Indians to make more black pots, since they were quite familiar with the mistake which caused them. Once Maria discovered that her pottery was even more popular than it had been formerly, she taught her sisters how to control this accident to satisfy the whites' taste. Eventually the rest of the women of the Pueblo were following her example. Maria's fame brought more tourists and more customers, so that everybody profited. Today San Ildefonso is associated with black pottery instead of red. The transformation of an informal, occasional black pot into a technical change in pottery making had other striking results. First it improved the over-all quality of the pottery of the Pueblo.

Then this change led to additional experimentation with pottery designs and finishes and opened the way for deviations from old patterns, which even led to the making of silver jewelry, traditionally associated with the Navajo and the Zuñi.

This example highlights a number of things about technical changes:

They are always specific. In this case one makes a choice as to the type of firing, one step in about a hundred steps needed to make a pot. Technical changes are readily observed, talked about, and transmitted to others. They open the way for additional changes and often improvement in the quality of a product. They often fly in the face of older formal norms and are far-reaching in their effects. Put together, they form the basis for a new formal system once they become consolidated and widely accepted.

Our own calendric system is an example of a once technical innovation, the result of many, many small technical changes built into a pattern that became widely accepted, so widely accepted that such periods as the hour and the week are thought of as "natural" divisions of time. In fact, it is so much a formal system that when the calendar was brought up to date in England in 1752 by gearing it to the Gregorian version, there were riots in the streets and people shouted, "Give us back our fourteen days."

To this point we have been looking at the formal-informal-technical triad as a fixed and static system. In actuality these states are constantly fluid, shifting one into the other—formal activity tends to become informal, informal tends toward the technical, and very often the technical will take on the trappings of a new formal system. In this next section I suggest something of the inherent processes by which these changes occur.

THE PROCESS OF CHANGE

Theodosius Dobzhansky, the great human geneticist, once observed that life was the result of neither design nor chance but the dynamic interaction of living substance with itself. He meant that life, in a changing environment, places such strains on the organism to adapt that, if this does not take place constantly, the organism as a species dies out. This process of adaptation leads to the production of the many complex forms that inhabit this earth. Different cultures are analogous to different species in the sense that some of them survive while others perish. Some are more adaptive than others. The study of change, therefore, is the study of survival. It is of more than academic interest, then, to see how the formal, informal, and technical exist in a relationship of continuous change. The theory of the nature of these relationships is a theory of change.

Because of the technical nature and complexity of the most available data I am including only one description of a changing culture pattern. (Three others will be found in Appendix III.) Its timeliness will be immediately recognizable, and it has in it many basic elements illustrating the principles by which culture change operates. It should be apparent to the reader that much of the material included under other headings also illustrates how change takes place.

An often noted characteristic of culture change is that an idea or a practice will hold on very persistently, apparently resisting all efforts to move it, and then suddenly, without notice, it will collapse. The following case history, well known to most Americans, is a poignant illustration of this phenomenon.

Taken at any given point, culture seems to be made up of formal behavior patterns that constitute a *core* around which there are certain informal adaptations. The core is also supported by a series of technical props. A classic case was provided one time during a discussion I had with a class of young college women. They were earnestly concerned with their future role in life. A topic very much on their minds, of course, was the matter of their relations with men. In a discussion of this subject one of the women summarized the issue very succinctly and at the same time illustrated the principle outlined above.

The problem she posed went as follows: Her family principally her mother, had endowed her with a series of formal beliefs which stressed the importance of premarital chastity. The young woman did not want to violate these beliefs, yet here she was, riding around in cars at night alone with boys, petting, and going to unchaperoned house parties. In effect, the traditional supports (or restraints) on which sexual virtue had long been based had been cut away. Moreover, there was continual pressure on her to chuck the idea of premarital chastity. How, she asked, could she maintain her position in the absence of supports? How could she preserve the core of a formal system when all of the important technical props had been removed?

In retrospect we can laugh at the thousand and one little props which once made it easy for a woman to keep her virtue. But how useful they were. I remember hearing an elderly New England lady who criticized her daughter-in-law about the way in which she handled her body, especially her legs. Her admonition went somewhat like this: "My dear, in this family a woman never crosses her legs. She sits forward on her chair with her head erect, her hands folded in her lap, and her knees together. On informal occasions, in the home and in the presence of her father or her brothers, she may cross her ankles." Today this sort of talk seems quaintly comical.

There used to be a separate vocabulary for men and

women. There were words that women were never supposed to hear. There were different postures and dress for the two sexes, and there were areas that were taboo to women—areas where they might not receive respectful treatment. Clothes hid everything but the face. Close chaperonage and limited times and places where young women could be seen with a man were enforced. All this occurred within the memory of a great many people living today.

In Latin America, however, the technical props which support formal virtue are still firm and elaborate. Americans have come to hold the view that the controls exist in the person and not in the situation. The Latin countries to the south make a different assumption. A man is thought of as being incapable of resisting his libidinal impulses in the face of a woman *if* the situation is such that he can succeed. Women are conceived of as frail creatures who could not possibly stand up to any man. Thus the situation has to be controlled with the full force of custom.

Obviously any change in the sexual manners of South America will have to hinge on a new conception of the nature of man and woman. This may already be coming about as more and more Latin women are being brought into contact with men in other than purely formal social relationships. A stenographer working in an office in daily contact with men is viewed very differently from the old-style well-chaperoned girl.

The differing rate at which formal and technical systems change, however, can lead to a good deal of personal anxiety. In sex the technical props have gone first in the United States, but the fact that the formal belief still stands is manifest in the question posed by the student and many others like her. How long it can stand is questionable. A few years ago G. P. Murdock, a famous anthropologist, was reported as saying that premarital chastity would not last another generation. People were appalled. He was attacked in the press, bombarded with angry letters, and condemned. The reaction was typical of what happens when someone predicts the collapse of any formal system.

Often technical systems turn into formal ones so quickly that people react to them as though they were still technical. Much of the workshiping at the shrine of scientific methodology in the social sciences these days smacks more of a formal system than a technical one. In these times it seems to be remarkably easy for scientists to turn into priests. Though unlike the ordained priest who knows he is a priest and receives the backing of a formal organization, the ritualistic scientist is engaged in a disconcerting masquerade.

A good example of this transition is what has happened to the psychoanalytic disciples of Freud in this country. Their operations have all the trappings of a religion, including the laborious re-examination of matters of dogma and a sort of excommunication for heretics. Many of them function very well within the system and manage to adapt because they know it's a formal system they are in—not a technical one. It is time, however, that we began to realize that much of what passes for science today may have been scientific yesterday but can no longer qualify because it does not make any additional meaningful statements about anything. It blindly adheres to procedures as a church adheres to its ritual.

Sometime in the future it will be possible to say more about the two types of technical statements which presume to be scientific. Type A seems to be designed to support a going concern and provides a prop for the formal core (laws, statements about conduct and ritual, regulations, and the like), while type B often does just the opposite, tearing down existing props and building new ones in their place. Men like Darwin, Newton, and

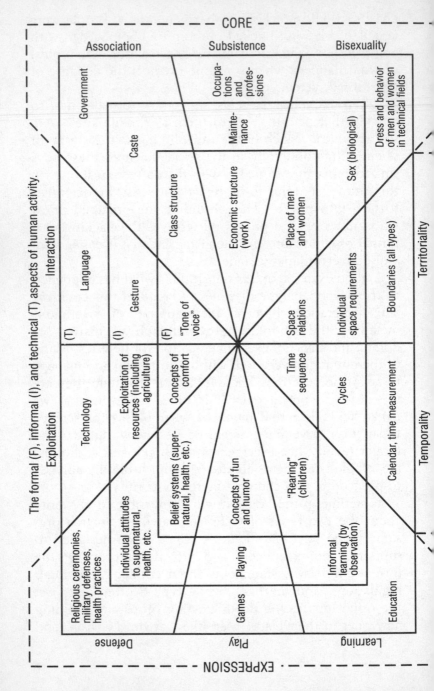

The formal (F), informal (I), and technical (T) aspects of human activity.

Einstein toppled old structures, clearing the way for new systems of thought. Type B tends toward the classic goal of true science, which is to explain more and more events with fewer and fewer theories. This contrast between the two aspects of the technical can best be summarized with the statement that *all scientific statements are technical, but not all technical statements are scientific.*

In summary, change is a complex circular process. It proceeds from formal to informal to technical to new formal, with the emphasis shifting rather rapidly at certain junctures. The rapid shifts are explained by the fact that people cannot tolerate existing in two systems at the same time; they have to approach life at any given moment from one of these three levels of integration but not more than one.

It is doubtful that anyone ever really changes culture in the sense that this term is ordinarily used. What happens is that small informal adaptations are continually being made in the day-to-day process of living. Some of them work better than others. These adaptations eventually become technicalized as improvements, and the improvements accumulate imperceptibly until they are suddenly acclaimed as "break-throughs." Steady, small improvements in airplane design have snowballed into machines undreamed of twenty years ago.

If a person really wants to help introduce culture change he or she should find out what is happening on the informal level and pinpoint which informal adaptations seem to be the most successful in daily operations. Bring these to the level of awareness. Even this process can only accelerate change, not actually control it in the manner desired by people of action. This is because the out-of-awareness nature of the informal is where all changes start. To paraphrase Dobzhansky, life is due to the dynamic interaction of living substance with itself and is not the result of either chance or design.

5

Culture Is
Communication

In recent years the physicist, the mathematician, and the engineer have accustomed themselves to looking at a wide range of events as aspects of communication. A book title such as *Electrons, Waves and Messages* does not seem incongruous. Another book title, *The Mathematical Theory of Communication*, seems so appropriate that it is readily accepted, at least by the scientifically inclined layperson. However, the behavioral scientists have only recently begun to examine their respective fields as communication.

The reader may wonder about the nature of the relationship between communication as I use the term and the communication theory (information theory) of the electronics laboratory. In one way it might be said that the communication theory is shorthand for talking about communication events that have already been subjected to considerable analysis, such as the phonetics of a language, orthographies, telephone and television signals, and the like. This process inevitably seems to proceed in one direction—toward symbolization. It must be remembered that when people talk they are using arbitrary vocal symbols to describe something that has happened or might have happened and that there is *no necessary connection between these symbolizations and what occurred.* Talking is a highly selective process because of the way in which culture works. No culture has devised a means for talking without highlighting some things at the expense of some other things. It follows that writing is a symbolization of a symbolization. Communication theory takes this process one step farther. The principal difference, as I see it, between the electronic engineer's approach and the approach of the cultural-communication specialist is that one works with highly compressed symbolic data while the other tries to discover what happens when people talk, before the data is stripped of all its overtones.

When considering all life as communication we see a spectrum covering a wide range of communication events. It is possible to observe complete messages of differing duration, some of them very short (less than a minute) and others covering years and years. In general the study of culture deals with events of fairly short duration. The psychology of the individual in cultural and social settings presents communication events of longer over-all duration. The study of government and political science may involve "messages" that take years to unfold. The following examples show how the duration of these messages can vary over a wide spectrum.

When a husband comes home from the office, takes off his hat, hangs up his coat, and says "Hi" to his wife, the way in which he says "Hi," reinforced by the manner in which he sheds his overcoat, summarizes his feelings about the way things went at the office. If his wife wants the details she may have to listen for a while, yet she grasps in an instant the significant message for her;

namely, what kind of evening they are going to spend and how she is going to have to cope with it.

Or take the example of a salesman who has been trying to sell something to an important client for a number of months. The client finally agrees to take up the business with his board of directors and promises to let the salesman know the verdict in a week. The first half second of the interview that follows usually tells the salesman what he wants to know—whether he has been successful or not.

A political figure makes a speech which is supposed to be reassuring. It has the opposite effect. When the words are read *they* are reassuring. Yet the total message as delivered is not. Why? For the same reason that the wife and the salesman know what to expect. Sentences can be meaningless by themselves. Other signs may be much more eloquent. The significant components of a communication on the level of culture are characterized by their brevity as compared with other types of communication. By simply raising the pitch of the voice at the end of an utterance instead of letting it fade away, it is possible (in English) to change a statement of fact to a question. The fact that communication can be effected in so brief a time on the cultural level is often responsible for the confusion which so often occurs in cross-cultural exchanges.

As one leaves the cultural part of the spectrum and proceeds to the personality portion, the wave length increases. The analytic building blocks, instead of being sounds and the like, are whole interactions between people—mother and child, for instance. Thus first impressions may be wrong because neither person has had a chance to reveal himself fully in a brief period. As a whole, the personality comes through rather slowly and is only fully known after years.

The portion of the communications spectrum which

embraces political events is composed of units of much longer duration. Meanings must be found in the context of hundreds of years of history. In a total pattern, a government's white paper is not just another document; it may be the equivalent of a period or a semicolon or even a question mark at the end of a message that has been building up for years. The message is composed of numerous situations and acts—something which is understood by any political scientist or statesman. Diplomacy and political strategy can be seen as a kind of debate where the words cover years.

Beyond this, scholars like Toynbee have been trying to work out the grammar of a message which may last for several hundred years, thereby transcending the lifetime of an individual human being. They analyze the syntax of whole societies and civilizations.

The trouble that social scientists have when they talk to someone who has been working on a different part of the communications spectrum is that what one sees clearly may be a diffuse blur or a microscopic dot to the other. Yet each researcher is trying his or her best to establish a pattern for extracting the meaning from what she/he studies. In the end all these patterns are relevant to one another. The language of politics and the language of culture are a long way apart, yet each subsumes the other.

Like a telephone system, any communication system has three aspects: its over-all structure, comparable to the telephone network; its components, comparable to switchboards, wires, and telephones; and the message itself, which is carried by the network. Similarly, messages can be broken down into three components: sets (like words), isolates (like sounds), and patterns (like grammar or syntax). A breakdown of messages into these components, sets, isolates, and patterns is basic to understanding culture as communication. A good deal of what follows is an explication of these terms and what lies behind them.

To recapitulate, people are constantly striving to discover the meaning of relationships between individuals and groups of individuals. The professional scholar soon learns to disregard the immediate explicit meaning of the obvious and to look for a pattern. Scholars also have to learn to scale perceptions up or down, depending upon what type of communication they are trying to unravel. This leads to an understandable occupational blindness which makes it almost impossible to pay close attention to communications of other types, on other wave lengths, as it were. An ability to decipher communications in a restricted area of specialization is what makes people experts. One person may be an expert in long-range events, another in short-term interactions. Further, if we return to language as it is spoken (not written) as a specialized communication system, we can learn something of how other less elaborated systems work. Most of what is known about communications has been learned from the study of language. Because the work with language has been so fruitful, there are certain analogies drawn from it which can be useful in the description of other communication systems.

In the study of languages, one can safely assume nothing. No two languages are alike; each has to be approached afresh. Some are so dissimilar, English and Navajo, for example, that they force the speaker into two different images of reality. Yet, whether a language is near or far, closely related or unrelated, there are certain steps which have to be taken in the analysis of the language in order that learning may proceed.

At first the new language is nothing but a blur of sound. Soon, however, some things seem to stand out, recognizable events recur. There are, for instance, perceived breaks or pauses, spaces which set off one event from another. It is usually assumed that these breaks separate words. Actually, they may be words, or they may be sentences, or they may be something else. The point is that there is something which is perceived, and this is what the learner grasps. For the time being we will call the things which we perceive "words." This is only a convenience, however, because the word as we know it is very limited in meaning.

In learning the new language, we discover, after having reproduced a number of words in our mouths, that the "words" are made up of sounds of various sorts, many of which are quite different from the sounds of English. Then we find that there is a way of stringing the words together that constitutes a complete utterance which we think of as a sentence.

To repeat, in discovering how a new language works and in learning that language, one starts with something akin to the *word*, made up of *sounds*, and put together in a particular way and according to certain set rules, which we call syntax. These are the basic steps and they identify the basic components of a language.

Because the terminology of the linguist is specialized and overly complex, Trager and I introduced a new set of terms which apply to all types of communication, including language. The cover terms are used to designate the three principal elements of a message. These are: *sets*, *isolates*, and *patterns*. The sets (words) are what you perceive first, the isolates (sounds) are the components that make up the sets, while the patterns (syntax) are the way in which sets are strung together in order to give them meaning.

The idea of looking at culture as communication has been profitable in that it has raised problems which had not been thought of before and provided solutions which might not otherwise have been possible. The fruitfulness of the approach can be traced to the clear distinction which was made between the formal, informal, and the technical, as well as the realization that culture can be analyzed into sets, isolates, and patterns. It is interesting to note that the early studies of the material culture of the American Indian were originally approached in this way but became entangled in a methodological bog because the study of linguistics had not progressed sufficiently at that time to enable the worker to draw any useful analogies from the way in which language worked. The data suggested, however, that there were things like the isolate which were called traits and catch-all combinations comparable to the word which were called trait-complexes.

In many instances the earlier attempts at handling material culture foundered because the living informant, if available at all, was not used properly to provide a true basis for the field worker's analysis. Somehow field work tended then, as it does today, to become contaminated by the culture of the scientist.

Like the philosophers and alchemists of the past who looked for the right things in the wrong way, many anthropologists have been searching for the essential building blocks of culture. Using the phoneme (the building block of language) as a model, they tried to discover its cultural equivalent, assuming in the process that culture was an entity, like language. Many of these efforts were based on incomplete understanding of the phoneme. In reality the phoneme is a cluster of sounds recognizable to the speakers of the language. The *a* as the New Englander pronounces it in the word "father," as well as its other regional variations, constitutes one phoneme. The *p* at the beginning of "pip" or "pop" is actually different from the *p* at the end, yet they are both known as allophones (recognizable variants) of the phoneme *p*.

The phoneme, like all other isolates, is an abstraction that dissolves into a set as soon as it is pinned down.

Since this was not understood by anthropologists, the phoneme did not provide a proper model for the rest of culture. The phoneme also represents just one structure point in a highly specialized communication system. It never pays to draw an analogy on the basis of structure points alone without reference to how the whole system behaves. When choosing building blocks such as phonemes as models, social scientists must be consistent. That is the concept of phoneme is imbedded in the context of a linguistic system and its function in that system must be understood. It seems that linguistic analysis requires some adaptation before it constitutes a suitable model for the other systems of culture. The subsequent chapters will be devoted to an expansion of what is meant by the terms isolate, set, and pattern, which are used to replace the terms phoneme, morpheme, and syntax as used in linguistics.

6

THE PERVASIVE SET

As a general rule, a set is a group of two or more constituent components that is perceived as being set apart from other events. Material objects such as chairs, tables, desks, and myriad other assemblages of things can be considered sets. So can words, periods of time, special measurements like the mile, and governing bodies, to mention only a few of the less tangible appurtenances of life which fit our definition. Because there are different types of sets, however—formal sets, informal sets, and technical sets—some sets are perceived more easily than others. Formal sets, for example, are those things which people take for granted and which seem natural: words, buildings, governments, families, the day, the months, and the year. Yet all these dissolve as satisfactory sets once one begins to look at them technically. We cannot think of words without languages, buildings without a civilization, time without periods.

Regardless of the level, sets are seldom perceived in isolation. Normally they appear in context and as one of many in a series of similar or related events. In the cross-cultural situation the first thing that a person will learn about another society is the existence of certain formal sets. These are either pointed out right away or they are so obvious that they cannot be missed. Yet in many cases newcomers never get beyond this first step. For example, they may learn a great many words (or sets) of a foreign language but still use the linguistic isolates of their mother tongue—which gives them an accent. Moreover, they may, without knowing it, fit the foreign words into the constructions, or patterns, of their native tongue— which can render their thoughts unintelligible. To take another example, we in America perceive all makes of cars as automobiles, whereas in certain parts of the Arab world only one make, the Cadillac, is considered an automobile. In such cases the foreigner (i.e., an Arab) feels he or she has mastered a set quite different from the ones he or she is familiar with and has the illusion of having understood another culture. In reality only the first hesitant step has been taken. To master a foreign culture it is necessary to master its patterns and isolates as well as its sets.

Sets are limited only by the number of possible combinations of their isolates and patterns. To try to deal with a foreign culture by learning more and more sets is a hopeless task. To collect sets in your mind is easy, but to decipher a pattern is difficult. Talking about sets without bringing in patterns is like talking about bricks without saying anything about houses. Thus, though this chapter is primarily devoted to sets, it is necessary to introduce the concept of pattern frequently.

If people can recognize a pattern, it doesn't much matter what specific events they perceive. These can, in fact, be quite different and still be part of the same pattern, just as houses are still houses even though made of different materials. Throughout the Middle East, for example, bargaining is an underlying pattern which is significantly different from the activity which goes under that name in our culture. Yet what is perceived on the surface (i.e., Arab methods of bargaining) looks familiar and is assumed to be the same. Nothing could be farther from the truth. Our first mistake is in the assessment of the value of bargaining in the Middle East and the role it plays in everyday life. Americans tend to look down on people who haggle. They restrict their serious trading to houses and automobiles. To the Arab, on the other hand, bargaining is not only a means of passing a day but actually a technique of interpersonal relations. However, it is not just the value placed on bargaining that is different in the Middle East but the pattern as well.

What we perceive on a first visit to an Arab country is a series of interactions that we recognize as something akin to bargaining. That is, we perceive the sets: the actions, the motions, the rises in the tone of voice, increases in loudness, the withdrawal, the handling of the merchandise. With all this going on before our eyes we do not ordinarily reflect on how our own pattern differs from this ostensibly familiar one. The American asks, "What percentage of the asking price shall I give as my first offer?" What he/she doesn't know is that there are several asking prices. Like the Eskimo who has many different words for snow, the Arab has many different asking prices, each with a different meaning. The American pattern is that the two parties have hidden prices above and below which they will not go, and an asking price which is perceived and thought of as having some sort of fixed relationship to the hidden prices. A more detailed analysis of how this all works will be discussed in Chapter Eight.

To return to sets, the principal point to remember is that they are the first thing to be observed, their number is unlimited, and the interpretation of their significance depends upon a knowledge of the patterns in which they are used.

There are additional generalizations which one can make about sets, however. These can be of use to the field worker, for they point the way to deeper patterns.

A large part of the vocabulary of a culture is devoted to sets. By looking at the vocabulary you can get a rough idea of the content of a culture and the things that are valued. The fact that we have only one word for snow while the Eskimos have several is a case in point. A highly developed technical vocabulary reflects a technical culture. Americans think nothing of having their advertising filled with words once known only to scientists and engineers, such as chlorophyll, thermonuclear, chloromycetin, cardiovascular, and the like.

The same set may be *valued* differently. The Latin American is likely to ask, if he comes from a place like Venezuela, why we emphasize something so dirty and unpleasant as plumbing. The Venezuelan may even want to know why we put the toilet in the bathroom. In Japan, to take another example, emotion or feeling is ranked very high. They call it *kimochi* or *dojo*. Logic, as we think of it, is ranked low. Our ranking of these two sets is, of course, almost the reverse of the Japanese.

Comparable sets are also composed of different components in different cultures. We think of a set of china as being primarily the dishes, cups, and saucers made from the same material and bearing the same pattern or in the same style. In Japan this does not hold. One of the many sets which I saw in the modern department stores in the Ginza was a "coffee set" in a box. It included five cups, five saucers, five spoons (all china), one aluminum percolator (kitchen variety), one cut-glass cream pitcher, and one plain sugar bowl with a plastic top. In the United States, no stretch of the imagination could put these diverse items in the same set.

Another important point is that the same sets are *classified differently* as one moves about the globe. This provides us with some additional stumbling blocks and gives us the illusion that we are really learning something different. In English, nouns are not classified as to sex. In Arabic, they are. You have to know the sex of the noun if you are to use it properly. We, on the other hand, classify everything into animate and inanimate, which would mean that Trobriand Islanders who do not make these distinctions would have to remember every time they referred to something whether we thought it was alive or not. They would also experience some difficulty with our animal and vegetable classifications, because they conceive of vegetables as being like animals and able to migrate from one garden to the next. (A good gardener to them is like a shepherd who is able to keep his or her own vegetables home and possibly even to entice a few, but not too many, of a neighbor's vegetables to enter his garden.)

English also has mass and non-mass nouns. Mass nouns comprise such things as sand, snow, flour, and grass. They are indicated by the phrase, "Give me some ———." Non-mass nouns include such objects as man, dog, thimble, and leaf. The phrase, "Give me a ———" is the linguistic clue to their existence. The foreigner always has to learn, pretty much by rote, which nouns are mass and which are not. Grass is, leaf isn't; there is no known consistent logic as to why a noun exists in one category and not another. In fact, it is true of sets generally that there is a good deal of plain old repetitious learning involved in their use. Vocabulary, wherever and however you find it, always has to be memorized.

We also distinguish between the various states of things—that is, whether they are active or passive. How the person speaking relates to natural events also varies. We say, "I'll see you *in* an hour." The Arab says, "What do you mean, 'in an hour'? Is the hour like a room, that you can go in and out of it?" To him his own system makes sense: "I'll see you before one hour," or "I'll see you after one week." We go out *in* the rain. The Arab goes *under* the rain.

Not only are sets classified, but they are broken down into further categories. An analysis of the number of sets in a given category can sometimes tell you the relative importance of an item in the over-all culture. The first person to speak scientifically about this trait was Franz Boas in his discussion of such things as the Eskimo's use of several different "nouns" for the many states of snow. In our culture one can get some idea of the importance of women by examining the tremendous proliferation of synonyms for females, particularly the young ones—cupcake, doll, flame, skirt, tomato, queen, broad, bag, dish, twist, to mention only a few. Each indicates a different variety or a subtle distinction in the ranking scale.

An additional attribute of sets, indicated by the above, is that they are almost always ranked within their category. The ranking, of course, varies as one moves about. White men at one time were ranked above Blacks in the United States. In Liberia it's the other way around. In fine watchmaking, gold is ranked above steel when elegance or social display is the goal. If one is a sportsman, steel may take precedence. To the American public as a whole, Cadillac ranks above Buick, which ranks above Chevrolet.

As a matter of fact, the ranking of sets is so subtle that one has to be more specific. It is not enough to say that sets are ranked. The categories of rankings, which reveal a pattern themselves, are of equal importance. In essence there are three different ways in which the set is ranked: (a) formally as a traditional item in a system of valued sets (lead, copper, gold, platinum); (b) informally, according to the taste of the observer or the demands of a situation (rare, medium, well-done steaks; red, green, blue, yellow); (c) technically, as points in a pattern: "Potatoes are selling for $5.00 a lot; yesterday they went for $4.95." The pattern in this case is the so-called law of supply and demand. On the Trobriand Islands a comparably comestible item like the yam was valued according to a completely different pattern. It was ranked according to its size, shape, when it was harvested, and who was to receive it. Supply and demand had nothing to do with the case.

Americans treat colors informally as a whole—that is, situationally. We may use a spot of yellow or of red, or yellow and red to accent a gray wall. We would be unlikely to put the yellow and the red next to each other. The colors in themselves have little or no value. If they do the criterion is taste. To the Navajo the situation is quite different; colors are ranked just as we rank gold and silver—only more intensely. Not realizing this caused considerable embarrassment to a number of Indian Service employees years ago. In their attempt to bring "democracy" to the Indians these well-meaning souls tried to introduce a system of voting among the Navajo. Unfortunately a great many Navajo were illiterate, so someone conceived of the bright idea of assigning the various candidates for the tribal council different colors so that the Navajo could go into the booth and check the color he or she wanted. Since blue is a good color and red bad, the result was to load the dice for some candidates and against the others. Nowadays photographs are used on the ballots.

Though Westerners tend to be impressed by big numbers and have an aversion to thirteen, one number is as good as the next now that superstition has dwindled away. Numbers only become meaningful in a technical context. The Japanese, however, have numbers that mean good luck, wealth, bankruptcy, and death. This fact complicates the Japanese telephone system. Following the war, good numbers brought a high price, unlucky ones were palmed off on foreigners.

It is quite clear then that one of the readily perceivable differences between cultures is the category to which a set is assigned and, once it is assigned, how it is treated: formally, informally, or technically.

In summary, we might point out that the only meaning which can be assigned to sets as sets is what we can call *demonstrational* meaning: This is a "dog"; that is a "man"; there goes an "airplane." By themselves, sets are neutral. In patterns, on the other hand, sets take on all sorts of more complex types of meaning. The most thorough analysis of sets in patterns has been carried on in the study of semantics, which is concerned with the meaning of words in various contexts. Though semantic studies have made remarkable progress they still have far to go. Their principal defect, as they are now conducted, is that the patterns are taken for granted.

7

THE ILLUSIVE ISOLATE

If the set is that aspect of existence which is most readily perceivable and the pattern is the organizational plan which gives it meaning, *the isolate is an illusive abstraction*, almost a phantom. It is the element which goes to make up a set, yet, paradoxically, the moment one begins to examine the set closely for its isolates the distinction between sets and isolates dissolves. To be sure, the isolates will reveal themselves, but as soon as they are clearly perceived, they are seen to be sets on their own level. This transition from set to isolate to set is of great importance. It has caused innumerable problems for the scientist, because when the transition occurs the whole perceptual structure changes. Even the old sets become something different. For example, a set which we call a "word" is perceived. Yet, when it is broken down into its component sounds which are the isolates, we find that the word as it was thought of originally has been lost forever. Every layperson has noticed this phenomenon when he begins to play with the sounds of a word, disregarding the word itself. When the linguists operating in a much more sophisticated fashion begin to record and classify sounds in their search for isolates, they realize that in addition to the usual vowels and consonants there are clusters of informal constants such as stress, pitch, and intonation. As a consequence, they are apt to find that the word does not break down and build up the way they thought it did. A series of new sets is perceived to take its place.

An analogue of the uncertainty principle of physics would seem to apply to this dilemma. The uncertainty principle holds that the observer and his/her instrument are inextricably bound up with the phenomena under observation and that the act of observation alters the conditions under observation. The more precisely our linguistic components are examined, the more abstract and imprecise the old observations become. In other words, when working with cultural data, *one can only be precise on one analytic level at a time and then only for a moment.* I call this "cultural indeterminacy."

When one considers the remarkable order repeatedly demonstrated by nature it is not surprising to discover that as soon as one starts looking for isolates in a given category of sets, like the sounds in words, certain recurrent uniformities appear. This fortunately puts definite limits to what otherwise might be an infinite job. One begins with the knowledge that what is being sought will ultimately turn out to be a discreet *category* of sets. In considering language, for example, one starts with the assumption that from a limited number of sounds all the words in English can be produced. We have also learned that there is a "sound *system*" for any language and that the speakers are *bound* by the system of their own language. This is why the first language one learns exerts an influence over all subsequent ones and gives them an accent. The binding effect of language is *not* in the sets but in the isolates and patterns. Almost anyone can reproduce the sounds of a foreign language in isolation, but many find that it is difficult to join them into a word. When they try it they alter the sound, so strong is the tie of old habits.

When the scientists, whatever their specialty, start their search for isolates, they know they will eventually find a *system* which will have an order and a pattern, and that this job will not last forever. There will come a time when they have mastered the system and can describe it. They can then teach people and by so doing create new systems, such as writing systems and alphabets and codifications of legal systems, to mention only a few of our intellectual constructs.

The goal of the investigator who deals with human phenomena is to discover the patterns of isolates that exist hidden in the minds, the sensory apparatus, and the muscles of people. These systems cannot ordinarily be discovered by using machines and precise measuring instruments. They have too much leeway in them and depend upon the capacity of humans to *recognize and respond to patterns*. If scientists are going to use machines, they must use them with tolerances that are appropriate to the data they are analyzing and the analytic level of analysis. If they are too precise, they turn up parts of systems which they are unable to handle. What is important are the distinctions the native speakers of the language make when they talk and those that they hear when they listen. These are the same. They make up a hidden system, the one shared with thousands, if not millions, of other people. The researcher is not concerned with individual variations, situational differences, dialects, nor speech defects but with the system that makes it possible for people to understand others even when they are missing important parts of their vocal apparatus, such as their teeth. What is wanted are the structure points around which behavior clusters and which are recognized as being related or thought to be the same. For we are looking for those things which enable all normal participants of a given culture (not 90 percent or 80 percent, but all) to distinguish between event A and event B. These events can be the conversation distance between two people, the waiting time on a street corner or antechamber, or, for that matter, anything in a culture that has meaning to the members of that culture.

Actually, to ask what it is that enables a person to tell the difference between A and B involves a different procedure from asking what goes to make up A and B. The difference in procedure is due to the fact that the subject cannot give a precise account of how he/she goes about making distinctions. But he/she can tell whether A and B are the same or different. The scientist's job is to analyze the difference and thereby uncover the hidden system of his subjects.

The procedure most commonly used is to work with the contrasting pairs of sets, taking up the differences pair by pair until all the distinctions have been identified. For example, pit is different from pat, tit different from tat. Since initial *p* sound and final *t* are held constant in pit and pat, the only variable is the short *i* and *a*. The same holds for tit and tat, bit and bat, and so on. With this information it is possible to construct a hypothesis that short *i* and *a* sounds are isolates and that speakers of the language will distinguish between them. Further, if one is substituted for the other in a word, the word will change. From this point on the scientist is faced with a good deal of routine drudgery. She/he continues his analysis, holding everything constant except the variable he/she is trying to pin down. A representative sample of the "words" of the language is worked through until it appears that all the significant distinctions made by native speakers have been identified. In spoken English there are 45 variables which combine to form all the sets and their combinations; 9 vowels, 3 semi-vowels, 21 consonants, 4 stresses, 4 pitches, and 4 junctures. There are only 26 variables—the 26 letters of the alphabet—used in the writing system, plus commas, periods, and question marks.

To summarize our discussion of isolates: It is quite clear that since they are, by definition, abstractions, isolates are difficult to describe. The concept of the isolate or the building block, however, seems to be an integral part of human communication on every level. Moreover, isolates are something mankind is constantly trying to discover and analyze, whether it is done consciously or not. The term isolate is also one which is used for convenience to denote the type of constituent event which goes to make up other events and is as much a designation of an analytic level as anything else. Despite their tendency to merge with one another, isolates and sets are firmly different in a good many respects. Isolates are limited in number, whereas sets are limited only by the possible patterned combinations of isolates. They are bound in a system and become sets only when they are taken out of that system. Sets, on the other hand, can be handled and perceived out of their systems but *derive their meaning* from the context in which they occur. Unlike the set which is clearly perceived, the isolate is an abstraction for events that cluster about a norm recognized by the members of a given culture. The actual difference between two isolates that are close to each other in the world of measurements may be less than the range of variation within the norm of each; it is the *pattern* in which they occur that enables man to distinguish between them. Speakers of the Mexican variety of Spanish, for example, can't distinguish between *i* as it occurs in "dish" and *e* as it occurs in "feet." For them, these are variants on the same sound. When they talk they don't know which they are reproducing.

The procedure for testing whether any given element in a grouping is an isolate is to hold everything constant and vary the element at will. If this changes the meaning of the grouping then the element is an isolate. The way one ends an utterance, for example, can make it either a statement or a question depending upon whether the voice falls or rises. Rising inflection at the end of the sentence is one isolate, falling inflection is another. This applies to English and some related languages but is not universal. A variant of this text is to note the one thing that keeps changing when everything else under observation seems to be constant. If this variation entails a change of meaning then the variable is apt to be an isolate.

Up to now the isolate has been described primarily as a constituent of the set. It is also one of the key elements in a pattern. Moreover, it can now be demonstrated that the basic work done on isolates which once seemed so trivial has been of crucial value in analyzing patterns. The isolate provides the transition from the set to the pattern *and is the principal means of differentiating between patterns*. This isolate, so hard to get at and to define, is now discovered to be the key to a great deal of the analysis of communication because it functions on three levels in three different ways: on the set level as a component part (c-a-k-e = cake); on the isolate level as a set (*each sound* is built up of parts) which the phonetician analyzes; on the pattern level as a differentiator of patterns. Thus the inability of a speaker to distinguish between initial *v* and *w* often patterns him/her as Scandinavian. Similarly, the transposition of the *oy* and *er* sounds in "oysters" and "birds" so that they come out as "ersters" and "boids" used to be a stereotype in most Americans' minds with native speakers of Brooklynese.

8

THE ORGANIZING PATTERN

Patterns are those implicit cultural rules by means of which sets are arranged so that they take on meaning.

Too little has been known about patterns and how they operate. True, the rules which hold for many aspects of culture could be quoted, but there was no theory of patterning, no account of how one analyzes and describes patterns.

In this chapter I shall make explicit a number of points which were only hinted at earlier. Some of these points cut quite deeply into our systems of belief and represent radical departures from our current ways of thinking and doing. The most basic is that there is no such thing as "experience" in the abstract, as a mode separate and distinct from culture. Culture is neither derived from experience nor held up to the mirror of experience. Moreover, it cannot be tested against some mystical thing thought of as experience. *Experience is something humans project upon the outside world as they gain it in its culturally determined form.*

Another series of basic points which I would like to stress is that there are laws governing patterns: laws of order, selection, and congruence.

The idea that people as cultural beings are bound by hidden rules and are not masters of their fates may come as a shock to some—it has always been hard to accept. The one thing that is quite clear, however, is that people are bound as long as they remain ignorant of the nature of the hidden pathways culture provides for them. To the traditional questions about free will, determinism, and his/her unique individuality which the ordinary citizen is apt to bring up when he/she meets the concept of a world of hidden rules, the anthropologist can give a convincing answer. Of course there are impulses that appear to have independent origins from within, but even these are radically altered by culture so that they are brought into play under controlled circumstances. The man who is attracted to a woman may want to invite her out for a date. The choice as to whether he acts or not is his. What is not his to decide fully is the language he will use, the presents he can give her, the hours he can call, the clothes he can wear, and the fact that in the United States the woman has the ultimate say in the matter. An American these days will not normally consider the revenge of the brothers as a price for seeing a woman without her family's permission, nor will it cross his mind that she might lose her life if she chooses to be intimate with him. These are not "alternatives" which occur to him as he is weighing the choice of patterns available to him. Death of the woman and revenge on the man are within the expected range of behavior in the less Europeanized parts of the Arab world. This sort of example is rather obvious and is the type of point which has been made many times and dismissed just as many times. Our rationalization is that it is "uncivilized" to kill one's sister just because she was intimate with a man. What we often don't know and have difficulty accepting is that such patterns fit into larger over-all patterns and that what is being guarded is not the sister's life (though she may be deeply loved) but a centrally located institution without which the society would perish or be radically altered. This institution is the family. In the Middle East the family is important because families are tied together in a functional interlocking complex. The accompanying network (and obligations) satisfies many of the same functions that our government satisfies. The sister is a sacred link between families and, like the judge in our own culture, she has to remain above reproach. Thus it is usually necessary to take a second look at the more obvious differences in behavior because they often hide or grow out of more fundamental differences that are just beginning to be studied: differences which control behavior in a way that was never dreamed of, that are not conventions implying a choice but rules that are so constant that they are not recognized as rules at all.

Benjamin Whorf, using language as the object of his investigation, had a good deal to say about the deeplying rules which control both thought and behavior. He was, in fact, one of the first to speak technically about the implications of differences which influence the way in which man experiences the universe. Until very recently it was believed that the thing that every person shared with others regardless of culture was *experience*. Yet it now seems doubtful indeed that experience is shared or that there is a *constant* that one can call experience in terms of which everything can be judged or measured. All cultures, rather, can be said to be relative to each other on the pattern level. There is a growing accumulation of evidence to indicate that mankind has no direct contact with experience per se but that there is an intervening set of patterns which channel his senses and his thoughts, causing him or her to react one way when someone else with different underlying patterns will react as *his* experience dictates.

Americans and Spaniards at a bullfight provide a familiar example of how the same set of circumstances can be experienced differently. The American experiences the fear he/she would have if he were in the ring; the Spaniard, vicariously, the joy in the control the matador exercises over the bull. Or take the brute fact of death as another example: Cora Du Bois, the well-known anthropologist, states that the people of Alor consider another person as dead long before Europeans would and often bury persons whom we consider still living. Ralph Linton, talking about the Tanala of Madagascar, describes how what we call death is conceived of as the assumption of a *new* status that involves active participation with the living. A woman has to get a divorce from her dead husband in order to marry someone else. To much of this the reader will say, "Yes, of course, but those people don't know any better, they are backward and ignorant and have no science. They haven't come as far as we have. What else can you expect of savages?" To this one can only answer, "Yes, but life and death are objective experiences and should therefore be the same—whatever the culture." The fact remains that they are not.

Whorf was concerned with the unconscious nature of the underlying assumptions upon which many of our actions are based. He develops this point in part in his article, "Science and Linguistics":

> We dissect nature along lines laid down by our native languages. The categories and types that we isolate from the world of phenomena we do not find there because they stare every observer in the face; on the contrary, the world is presented in a kaleidoscopic flux of impression which has to be organized by our minds—and this means largely by the linguistic systems in our minds. We cut nature up, organize it into concepts, and ascribe significances as we

do, largely because we are parties to an agreement to organize it in this way—an agreement that holds throughout our speech community and is codified in the patterns of our language. The agreement is, of course, an implicit and unstated one, *but its terms are absolutely obligatory;* we cannot talk at all except by subscribing to the organization and classification of data which the agreement decrees.

This fact is significant for modern science, for it means that no individual *is free to describe nature with absolute impartiality* but is constrained to certain modes of interpretation even while he thinks himself most free.

In another article titled "Linguistics as an Exact Science," Whorf continues:

. . . we all hold an illusion about talking, an illusion that talking is quite untrammeled and spontaneous and merely 'expresses' whatever we wish to have it express. This illusory appearance results from the fact that the obligatory phenomena within apparently free flow of talk are so completely autocratic that the speaker and listener are bound unconsciously as though in the grip of a *law of nature.* [Italics mine.]

The implications of these statements go very deep indeed. They mean for one thing that once we have begun to really understand another people by mastering their language, we will still find hidden barriers which separate one people from another.

Yet there is a way to hurdle these hidden barriers.

In terms of my earlier discussions of sets and isolates, the simplest definition of a pattern that one could arrive at was this: A pattern is a meaningful arrangement of sets. What is left unsaid here is that a pattern is only meaningful if analyzed on its own level. For instance, the linguist's phoneme is a meaningful arrangement of sets to the linguist but not to laymen. A tastefully decorated living room is a meaningful arrangement of sets to women who belong to the same group and who are aware of the art of decorating a room. Men are likely to look at the room as a set, to see it as one thing, and to respond to the overall effect. What they don't see, which many women do, is the detail. It is the detail in a pattern that tells one woman so many things about another. To most people a horse is a horse, yet a trainer experienced in the buying and selling of horses examines a number of sets such as height, weight, length of barrel, thickness of chest, depth of chest, configuration of the neck and head, stance, coat condition, hoofs, and gait. To the non-expert these characteristics are seen as isolates, but to the expert each isolate is seen in relation to all the rest. The total adds up to a pattern, a story or picture of the horse. That is, the expert places this horse into a pattern along with other horses that are similar, just as a winetaster evaluates the "qualities" of a wine. The important thing to remember is that the pattern is *seen* as a pattern only if it is examined on its own level and without leaving that level.

A given pattern is only obvious to certain categories of people. A man sees one thing in a room, a woman something else, a maid something else. This means there is a relationship between the people and patterns. In effect, groups can be defined by the relation of their members to a certain pattern. The individuals of a group share patterns that enable them to see the same thing and this holds them together. In the light of this analysis it is necessary to expand the definition of a pattern. It should now read: A pattern is a meaningful arrangement of sets shared by a group.

THE THREE TYPES OF PATTERNS

At the beginning of the century Japanese businessmen were coming to this country in increasing numbers. Like all travelers, they had difficulty orienting themselves. One of them is said to have written a book for other Japanese businessmen who might travel to America. In interpreting the passage that follows, it should be remembered that relative status is the key to much of Japanese life. This hierarchical system is formal, yet a great many of the rules are technical. It comes as no surprise, then, to find that our Japanese author opens his book by telling his readers that American life is full of ceremony but that the ceremony is so complex that no foreigner can ever hope to master it. Courageously, however, the writer offers a guide to conduct by instancing examples of behavior which might be followed. When two American businessmen meet, he points out, there is a lot of noise, they beat each other on the back, then as though by signal they both reach for cigars which they offer to each other. Both men will refuse the other's cigar, but ultimately the man of inferior status will accept the cigar of the man of superior status.

Despite this somewhat bizarre analysis, most of us recognize the pattern. It is an informal one which is dying out. But we also know that part of the pattern is that the senior will accept the cigar of the junior if the junior is on the way up—a cue to him that the "old man" recognizes this. The hierarchical emphasis which the Japanese observer gave this pattern suggests another aspect of our way of life which is ostensibly characterized by an underlying formal pattern of equality. It points up to the fact that we also have a very complex informally patterned status system. The counters on the mobility scale are numerous and so finely grained that while the average person can manipulate the system he/she cannot describe how it works technically. Many recent American novels such as *The Man in the Gray Flannel Suit* have tried to describe one segment of this system. Status, as a matter of fact, is a persistent thread running through the American novel. One theme is to play on the conflict between informal ranking system and the basic equality pattern. Another deals with characters who rise too fast, find themselves caught in unfamiliar patterns, and are penalized for their unfamiliarity.

Formal patterns in America hold that when we want to express joy we laugh, to express grief we cry. They insist, moreover, that it is much easier for women to laugh and cry than for men. In Japan, as many an American discovered, laughter does not always mean that a person is happy. It may mean that he is embarrassed. Crying, too, may not necessarily mean that a person is sad. Whenever the social scientist tries to illustrate formal patterns and is of necessity restricted to a bit of a communication torn out of context, he has to deal with people who take great pleasure in saying such things as, "Oh yes, but in the United States people cry when they are happy too." This is quite true. But the fact is that we think it is "natural" to cry when sad and laugh when happy. Luckily, as I have pointed out, formal patterns often offer a great deal of leeway in the way in which they can be expressed. The boundaries are usually well known by everyone concerned, and as long as they are not violated there is considerable range of variation allowed. The principal difference between the German and the Austrian illustrates this point. The Germans tend to be more technical in the restrictions they place upon themselves than the Austrians, who are more formal. The result is that the Austrian appears to be much more easygoing. They are more relaxed about most things, which gives them somewhat more freedom, providing, of course, that they stay within certain well-prescribed limits. Americans, on the other hand, have comparatively few technical and formal restrictions placed upon them but are loaded with informal ones. This means that Americans are apt to be quite inhibited, because they cannot state explicitly what the rules are. They can only point to them when they are violated.

I have already touched upon the differences between the United States and the Middle East in the art of bargaining. The example is worth further elaboration. The American pattern of bargaining is predicated on the assumption that each party has a high and a low point that is hidden (what he/she would like to get and what he/she will settle for). The function of the bargaining is to discover, if possible, what the opponent's points are without revealing one's own. The American in the Middle East, projecting his own unconscious pattern, will ask, "What percentage of the asking price do I give?" That is, "If they ask for ten pounds, will they settle for five?" This procedure is not only wrong but can end in trouble. The principle to be remembered is that instead of each party having a high and low there is really only *one* principal point, which lies somewhere in the middle. Much like our latest stock market quotation, this point is determined, not by the two parties, but by the market or the situation. An important isolate in this pattern is that the price is never determined by the person or his/her wishes but always by some set of circumstances which are known to both parties. If they are not known it is assumed that they could be. Negotiation, therefore, swings around a central pivot. Ignorance of the position of the pivot opens one up to the worst type of exploitation, as well as loss of face. It doesn't matter whether it is a squash in the bazaar or a hydroelectric dam in the international market. The pattern remains constant. Above and below the central point there is a series of points which indicate what the two parties feel as they enter the field.

Here is how an Arab from Damascus described this process. The pivotal point was six piasters, the price of squash on the day he described. Above and below this there were four points. Any one of the top four might be the first price asked by the seller. Any one of the lower four represents the first offer made by the prospective buyer. The hidden or implicit meaning of this code is given opposite each step on the scale below. This meaning is not exact but represents a clue as to the attitudes of the two parties as they enter the bargaining process.

Piasters

12 or more	complete ignorance on the part of the seller	Seller's asking prices
10.......	an insult, arguments and fights ensue, seller doesn't want to sell	
8........	will sell, but let's continue bargaining	
7........	will sell under the market	
6........	*market price (the pivot)*	
5........	buyer really wants the squash, will pay over the market	
4........	will buy	Buyer's offering prices
2........	arguments and fighting, buyer doesn't want to buy	
1........	ignorance of the value of the item on the part of the buyer	

Considering the difference of meaning which is carried by a variation of one piaster, the question, "What percentage of the asking price do I give?" seems meaningless. Which asking price? The let's-do-business one, the let's-not-do-business one, or the let's-fight asking price? Other variations on this pattern have as many as five or six points above and below the line, each with its own meaning.

One cannot underestimate the importance of such patterns and the hold they have on people at all levels. In discussing our stand in Egypt during and directly following the Aswan Dam fiasco and before our position in the Middle East had deteriorated so badly, an Arab sympathetic to our cause expressed it this way. "If you don't give a little in bargaining, the other fellow will back up. If he gives two steps, you have to give two steps. If you don't, he will back up four." We didn't give our two steps and Nasser backed up four.

When events of such magnitude may depend on such small understandings it seems clear that one of the most promising developments in the intercultural field has to do with research directed toward bringing informal patterns to awareness. In many ways this work is the most meticulous, painstaking, and difficult of all. Even the best of informants can never describe informal patterns though they have been born and raised in a culture and have all their wits about them. The scientists work in the dark, creating hypotheses about what they think are consistent behavior patterns and then tests the hypotheses until they are sure they have pinned one down. Work of this type is highly rewarding because of the genuine sense of discovery. Once an informal pattern has been adequately described it can then be understood by others in the same culture with almost lightning speed since it has already been acquired. By making it explicit all the scientist really does is to "put it in words," which will make it easier for informal patterns to be taught.

Much of the difficulty in our schools today stems from the fact the teachers try to inculcate and teach patterns that are partially or incorrectly analyzed. In many instances the technical descriptions simply do not fit the facts. Instead of having a familiar ring to the child there is a decidedly unfamiliar ring. In fact, much of what the child hears goes against everything he/she has learned outside the classroom. A good deal of the content taught under the rubric of "grammar" falls in this category. Take the "can" and "may" distinction that teachers spend so much time trying to instill in children. It would seem that this distinction originally developed informally and was linked to sex; men and boys said "can," women and girls "may." "May" naturally sounded more refined to the women so they insisted on foisting it on the men along with a lot of gobbledygook about possible and not possible. At the present time, what with the women trying to be like the men and the men doing more and more things women used to do, the may-can now is so mixed up it's almost impossible to develop any rules. It is possible for either to be applied in a great many situations.

The can-may distinction illustrates one of the many different types of informal patterns that exist in our language. Another type is associated with the use of what is technically known as the *superfix* first identified by Trager. The reader is familiar with prefixes and suffixes that are added at the beginnings and ends of stems. The superfix, as the word implies, goes over or above the utterance.

By identifying the superfix Trager raised a whole category of grammatical and other events from the informal to the technical. That ill-defined, highly significant agglomeration of vocalizations known as "tone of voice" began to be unraveled by identification of the superfix. The difference between an adjectival and a nominal is signaled by the use of superfixes, in this case varying degrees of loudness or stress. For example, in English the difference in the spoken language between green house (the color green), greenhouse (where plants are grown), and the Green house (house owned by Mr. and Mrs. Green) is solely a function of varying stress. The French, incidentally, do not share this pattern with us and cannot hear the difference between these three utterances. The new rules of grammar for English, when they eventually appear may describe adjectivals in terms of their stress pattern in relation to other items.

It would not be right to blame early grammarians because they did not analyze all the informal patterns of language or because much of what they did analyze fell short of the mark. We should distinguish, however, between the three types of patterns in order to help bolster our sagging educational system as well as for the peace of mind of our children. All three can be learned or taught but in entirely different ways. As has been said, the best way to learn an informal pattern is by selecting a good model and copying him as closely as possible. Formal patterns, as stated previously, are learned by precept and admonition. Technical ones are spelled out.

In addition to isolating the three principal types of patterns, Trager and I discovered that all seem to be bound by three laws: those of *order, selection*, and *congruence*. It should be emphasized that there may be additional laws governing the formation of patterns which have not yet been discovered. These three seem to provide a beginning.

ORDER

The laws of order are those regularities governing changes in meaning when order is altered. "The cat caught the mouse" means something obviously different from "The mouse caught the cat." A great sin in medieval times was the saying of the Black Mass in which the order of the service was reversed. Anyone who is a practitioner of any of the communicative arts is fully familiar with the effect of reorienting the sequence of words, sentences, and paragraphs. Below the sentence level, the order in which the sounds are put together is the basis of the formation of words. Words that mean the same thing whether you read them forward or backward are a pleasant aberration from the rule of verbal order, as are words which have a real meaning when read backwards. Order is used differently in different cultures. With us it is a basic part of our grammatical system. It should be noted that while order is of critical importance on the sentence level in English this is not the case in inflected languages like Latin and Old English of the time of Alfred. Order has great importance in other cultural systems besides language: order of birth, order of arrival, order in line to get tickets. Order applies to the courses of a meal. Consider what it would be like to start dinner with dessert, then switch to potatoes, hors d'oeuvre, coffee, salad, and end with meat.

Order permeates almost every activity in a culture like our own. Yet in some other cultures the activities in which order is important may represent basic pattern differences between cultures. American housewives who have had to train servants overseas are all too familiar with the difficulty of inculcating them with American ordering patterns, the order in which courses should be served, or the weekly schedule of household cleaning. Anyone who has listened to the ever-increasing number of Americans who have lived abroad has probably heard an anecdote in which a servant suddenly appears with a lighted birthday cake in the middle of a meal. In short, the placing of the climax of any event varies all over the world.

Understanding the variations in order is a major factor in overseas work. The American knows that in his or her own country the order in which people arrive at a restaurant is supposed to determine when they get served and the order in which they are hired dictates when they are laid off. To Americans, to be first is to be more deserving. If Americans have been sitting at a table in a restaurant for some time and a latecomer is served before they are, their blood pressure will rise noticeably. Yet in most places outside of Europe ordering in situations of this type is unknown. Instead the laws of selection apply; that is, service is dependent upon a person's rank.

Another type of order is that of societies like the Pueblo of New Mexico and Arizona where age (order of birth) determines prestige, status, respect, and deference. The essential point is that societies will order the *people*, or the *situation*, or a *station* in life but not all three simultaneously.

SELECTION

Selection controls the combination of sets that can be used together. We say *a* boy and *an* arm. Struck and stricken illustrate another case in which the rule of selection is seen to function. We say that he was "awe-struck" but also that he was "stricken dumb." We may be struck by a car, but we are always stricken with grief. There is no inherent logic to selection. The most one can say is that in such and such a case the selection works as follows and state the over-all category. Why, for instance, should we drive on the right and the British on the left? Like all the rest of culture, the selection patterns change with time. There was a time, for example, when men wore much more jewelry and more fancy clothing than they do now.

For every pattern there are certain points at which selection applies, just as there are other points at which order is brought into play. What enables us to differentiate between patterns is that they do not use selection and order in the same way.

Order has been mentioned as having an important part in our eating pattern. Selection also plays an important but different role. Breakfast usually consists of a number of items selected from a limited list of edibles: fruits and their juices, cereals in various forms, berries, bacon, sausage, eggs, pancakes, waffles, rolls, toast, butter, jelly or jam, and coffee, tea or milk. Depending on the region of the United States, certain other items can become part of this pattern—like grits in the South and pan-fried potatoes in the Middle West, for example. Steak and potatoes are still eaten for breakfast by a few New Englanders and by ranchers in the West in diminishing numbers. The list does not include châteaubriant, green turtle soup, or oysters Rockefeller.

Selection plays a prominent part in the patterns of social relations around the world in dress, sex, and in work and play—in fact, all of the basic primary message systems. The easiest way to determine when selection is being applied is to note whether there is something bound to something else by custom when any number of other items could "logically" serve the same purpose. The law of selection demands a white tie with tails. This law also demands the residence of a wife or female relative of the President in the White House. I chose the term selection for the very reason that something is "selected" out of a category. Once the selection has occurred it is arbitrarily binding. The arbitrariness of culture is generally not understood because there are other areas where culture has tremendous leeway. Selection is a major exception.

CONGRUENCE

Congruence is more difficult to talk about precisely than either order or selection. Its subtle dictates may, nevertheless, be more binding. Unlike order and selection, which have to do with the patterning of sets, the law of congruence can be expressed as a *pattern of patterns*. Congruence is what all writers are trying to achieve in terms of their own style, and what everyone wants to find as he/she moves through life. On the highest level the human reaction to congruence is one of awe or ecstasy. Complete congruence is rare. One might say that it exists when an individual makes full use of all the potentials of a pattern. Lincoln's Gettysburg Address is an example. Complete lack of congruence occurs when everything is so out of phase that no member of a culture could possibly conceive of himself creating such a mess.

Lack of congruence in dress is always obvious and often humorous—witness the endless 19th century cartoons of natives wearing a loin cloth and a silk hat. In architecture when Culture A borrows architecture from Culture B, Culture A takes the sets but not the pattern. Witness the outrageous Greek columns and detailing on any suburban mansion.

In many instances attempts are made to achieve congruence on one level without regard to distortions introduced on another. For example, schoolteachers are apt to criticize their charges for saying "most unique," their argument being that uniqueness is not a matter of degree. What is happening, of course, is that the teacher is borrowing a criterion from the level of logic and applying it to the level of language. Language, it so happens, works in such a way that any adjectival can have comparative and superlative degrees. In order to obtain complete congruity, however, the word unique can only be used in certain situations.

Many jokes are based on incongruities of one sort or another, which is one reason why the readers (or listeners) have to be almost a native speaker in order to appreciate the full implications of a joke. If they are unable to assess the degree of incongruity they can't appreciate the humor. The old joke about the girl from Brooklyn trying to put on airs in Schrafft's by ordering "esters on the half shell" (using a very Bostonian *a!*) is funny because it is incongruous on several levels. Not only does she use two dialects but switches from substandard usage to what she thinks is upper-class.

Pattern congruity or style in writing is a function of knowing what can and cannot be achieved within the limits of the pattern. Newspaper or journalistic writing is adapted to the medium and all that medium implies. When it is bad it's because the writer has not learned what can be done within the limits set by the pattern. To do this type of writing well is a highly skilled art and is learned only after years of experience. The writing of the scientist is often incongruous because it drags the reader from one analytic level to the next and then back again. Most scientific writing treats the reader like the boor who says "get it," indicating the scientist's fear that people will twist, distort, and take exception to what has been said. The scientist has to communicate on a number of different analytic levels at once by footnoting and overqualifying each statement. In defense of my fellow scientists it should be said that one of the most difficult things in the world to do is to learn to keep the levels apart as well as to maintain congruity. Harry Stack Sullivan, a very great contributor to psychiatric thinking in this country, once described his own attempts at writing by saying that the person who appeared before him as he wrote and who appraised his sentences as they were coming out was a cross between an imbecile and a bitterly paranoid critic! Sullivan was not alone in having this kind of self-image; he recognized the difficulties and the humor of having to try to force one's writing onto such a Procrustean couch. Another point to make about scientists is that most of them are more concerned about making precise statements than they are about writing. They depend upon their colleagues to know what they are talking about. Therefore, they can get by with less literary ability than writers. Scientific congruity and not literary congruity is their preoccupation.

There is one thing that seems quite certain. While people demonstrate varying degrees of sensitivity for congruence, perfect congruence is seldom achieved. It *lurks* in every culture and is captured by us only in rare creations. True artistry exists when congruence is so high that everything appears simple and easy, when it communicates so clearly that people wonder why they didn't say it themselves.

People toil to perfect congruence. They pay endless attention to details, to sets and the isolates, and to the overall pattern. Usually it is a matter of going over and over a statement and making it clearer and clearer so that finally everything fits and nothing comes between what is being communicated and the audience.

One might assume that much is known about pattern congruity. Actually the field has hardly been delineated as a field of scientific study. The principal difference between the concept of congruence and the more widely held beliefs about ecstatic productions is that traditionally the artists' productions are viewed as if they created the rules for their masterpieces without reference to the pattern of the culture. This is not to say that the artist has no control over what is "good" or "bad" art. They do. There is a close relationship between the person and the over-all pattern in which they participate. Some artists are more sensitive to lack of congruence than others and strive more strongly to reduce tensions induced by incongruity. Indeed, it is this tremendous sensitivity to pattern incongruity that the artists bring to their work. They have a highly developed sense for working within patterns, making the most of them, pushing and stretching their boundaries but never crossing them, so that the spell can be maintained and not broken. The artist likes to play with patterns and find out what really can be done with the material at hand. They sometimes do this in the context of small groups of people concerned with or interested in areas of culture stress, tension, and change. Because many artists are participating in variants of the overall pattern that are not widely shared, they often have the reputation for setting the pace for everyone else. They are credited with "creating" new patterns. Yet most artists know that what greatness they have lies in being able to make meaningful statements about what is going on around them. They say what others have tried to say but say it more simply, more directly, and more accurately, more incisively and with greater insight.

Artists do not lead cultures and create patterns; they hold up a mirror for society to see things it might not otherwise see. Proof that art reflects the culture and the times of the artist can be had by simply walking through any reasonably well-stocked museum or by looking at the illustrations in contemporary art books.

The "rule" of congruence, or style in the broadest sense, pervades not only the world of art but all kinds of communication. The present state of our understanding of how congruence works is so rudimentary, however, that we are barely able to provide evidence of faulty communications, much less specify what the faults may be. Yet in an international debate serious errors are made in interpreting such supposedly simple matters as whether one participant is actually angry or merely bluffing. No wonder there are wars! The sheer frustration of not being able to understand sometimes makes one want to strike out in the feeling that at least the blow will be understood. Yet it's quite obvious that we can do better than that; the drive toward congruity would seem to be as strong a human need as the will to physical survival. The study of culture is beginning to provide insights. It could do more, but what is encouraging is the development of the tools for understanding. Two of the most promising leads are in the study of patterns of the informal type and in developing our knowledge of congruence and how it functions.

9

TIME TALKS: AMERICAN ACCENTS

At the beginning of this book I offered a cursory analysis of time as an element of culture which communicates as powerfully as language. Since my conceptual scheme had not yet been developed in detail at that point my survey was rather sketchy. Now that I have presented the technical tools for probing the secrets of culture, I can return to time. Here I shall consider the way Americans use time and communicate by it, stressing the details and the subtleties which close analysis turns up. Some of the points I make may arouse a shock of recognition, a feeling that here is something which the reader knew all along. This is the way it should be. The analysis of one's own culture simply makes explicit the many things we take for granted in our everyday lives. Talking about them, however, changes our relation with them. We move into an active and understanding correspondence with those aspects of our existence which are all too frequently taken for granted or which sometimes weigh heavily on us. Talking about them frees us from their restraint.

A well-known authority on children in the United States once stated that it took the average child a little more than twelve years to master time. This estimate is probably somewhat conservative. Young people of this age know how our basic time system works but do not yet seem to have fully internalized either the details or the emotional overtones of the formal time system.

Why does it take a child so long to learn time? The answer is not simple. In fact, when one begins to discover how many complications are involved he or she may wonder whether the full range of subtleties of time can be mastered at all.

The three systems I have discussed—formal, informal, technical—often use identical items of vocabulary. This does not make it any easier for the child, or the foreigner, to learn them. The year, for instance, is a *formal* or traditional part of our time system. It means three hundred sixty-five days plus one fourth day which is accounted for by inserting leap year. It can also mean twelve months, as well as fifty-two weeks.

Informally, we may say, "Oh, it takes years to get that done." You have to be there and know the person and the background of the remark before you know exactly what his word "years" means. It may be a matter of minutes, weeks, or actual years. *Technically*, the year is quite another thing again. Not only is it counted in days, hours, minutes, seconds, but there are different types of years of different lengths. Minutes, hours, months, and weeks are also used in all three contexts. It is only the total context that tells us which type of time is being referred to.

Almost anyone can recapture that moment of his childhood when the day was almost spent and Mother was asked, "Mommy, how long will it be before we get home? I'm tired." And Mother replies, "Just a little while, dear. Now you just be good and before you know it we'll be home."

"How long is a while?" "It's hard to say, dear." "Is a while five minutes, Mommy?" "Sometimes, dear, but not always. In this case it will be a little longer than five minutes." "Oh."

At this point the child gives up—for the time being at least.

Not only are there three different categories of time, but each has its own subdivisions; its sets, its isolates, and its patterns, which make nine different types of time found for our culture. Fortunately, to simplify matters, laypeople do not need to know the whole technical system in order to get along. Yet they depend upon others to know it.

Laypeople, getting technical, may ask an astronomer exactly how long a year is. At which point they discover their own ignorance by being asked what kind of year they have in mind—the tropical or solar year (365 days, 5 hours, 48 minutes, 45.51 seconds plus a fraction); the sidereal year (365 days, 6 hours, 9 minutes, 9.54 seconds); or the anomalistic year (365 days, 6 hours, 13 minutes, 53.1 seconds).

Our formal time system is that part of the over-all system which we would not change and don't want others tampering with. Yet this formal system we take so much for granted was once a technical system known only to a few priests along the Nile who had perfected it in response to a need to forecast annual floods more accurately.

FORMAL TIME: SETS, ISOLATES, AND PATTERNS

A quick way to discover how our European time sets operate is to teach them to children. The day is a formal set deeply rooted in the past. It has two primary isolates, day and night, and is further broken down into morning and afternoon, punctuated by meals and naps, and other recurrent occasions. There are seven different categories of days: Monday, Tuesday, Wednesday, etc. They are valued differently, Sunday being set apart. The child is usually in control of these notions by the age of six. At eight most children learn to tell time by the clock. This process can be simplified for them if it is explained that there are two types of time (two categories of sets): hours and minutes. The hours—one to twelve—have to be learned so well that recognition is instantaneous. Before learning the minutes the children learn that the quarter hour is the isolate most useful to them. They can grasp these quite quickly: five-fifteen, five-thirty, and five forty-five begin to make sense. Minutes should not be taught as isolates first but as sets, of which there are sixty. However, to make life a little simpler since the child can't perceive a minute, these cluster together in five-minute periods; five, ten, and fifteen after the hour, right on up to five fifty-five. Finally, the two sets of sets are blended into one system.

In America any Easterner or urban Middle Westerner conversant with the way her or his own culture values time can perceive that five minutes is different from ten minutes. That is, the five-minute period is the smallest formal set. It has only recently crossed the boundary from isolate to set. Twenty years ago the five-minute period was an isolate of a particular type that went to make up the quarter hour. Now people are aware of whether they are five minutes late or not and will apologize.

In Utah the Mormons have developed promptness to a degree that is unknown in the rest of the country. In their system the minutes would seem to be an inviolate set. On the northwest coast the traditional feelings about time are altered and are not experienced in as pressing a manner as they are elsewhere. The Northwest uses the same time structure as the rest of the country, but nobody seems particularly driven by it. The main difference is that they lack the informal isolate of urgency.

Beyond the five-minute period there is the *ten*-minute period, the quarter hour, the half hour, and the hour. Then there is the morning divided into early, middle, and late; the noon hour; early, mid- and late afternoon; and evening, as well as similar divisions for the nighttime.

Formally, our day starts at midnight. The periods set off by meals and by sleeping and waking are probably the earliest of the perceived temporal sets for children. Television is speeding up the process of helping children to notice the difference between, say, five o'clock and six o'clock, since these are the times when their pet programs come on.

The week is also a set, introduced as a part of the Egyptians' technical time system. It is not, however, universally grasped. The term fortnight, like many other Anglo-Saxon survivals, remains present in the system, a reminder of earlier times. It is still used as the pay period in the government and as a publication period for certain periodicals. It is, however, a bit archaic and is slowly falling into disuse. The month, like the day, is a set that has been established as a component in our time system for a long time. It is used for payments and rendering of accounts, reports of almost every type, and jail sentences.

The season is both a formal set and an informal one. It is probably one of the oldest of our sets. It used to mark plowing, planting, cultivating and harvesting time, as well as the time when the soil could rest. Now, of course, there are hunting, fishing, skiing, tourist, or Christmas seasons, as well as the traditional summer, fall, winter, spring class of sets. The season and the quarter are probably related, although the quarter is tied to the calendar while the season, being older, is rooted in climatic changes and activities associated with agriculture.

Formal isolates are difficult to pin down. Like all isolates, they are abstractions, yet because they are formal abstractions which seem right and proper little attention has been paid to them. They are often overlooked because they seem so "natural."

The list of true isolates which follows is undoubtedly incomplete. It includes what I call ordering, cyclicity, synthesisity, valuation, tangibility, duration, and depth.

The week is the week not only because it has seven days but because they are in a fixed *order*. Ordering as a formal isolate would seem to be an expression of *order* as in the laws of order, selection, and congruence. The Western world has elaborated this to some extent. That is, we keep constant track of all sorts of things which are otherwise identical and *only distinguish between them because of their order*. The six millionth Ford built becomes a milestone, as does the fifty millionth passenger-mile flown by an airline. The first-born, first president, first position, the number-two man, the tenth in a class of one thousand assume meaning because of their order. The seventh day is different from the first day; the middle of the week is different from the end, and so on.

For most temporal events the *cyclic* element is taken for granted. One day follows the next, as does the week, month, year, and century. The common cycles are limited in number. The sixty-cycle series (minutes and seconds) the seven-day week, and the twelve-month year.

Valuation is expressed in our attitude that time itself is valuable and should not be wasted.

Tangibility is expressed in the fact that we consider time as a commodity. It can be bought, sold, saved, spent, wasted, lost, made up, and measured.

For people raised in the European tradition time is

something that occurs between two points. *Duration* is the most widely shared implicit assumption concerning the nature of time in the Western world. It seems inconceivable to those of us who have learned to take this one isolate so much for granted that it would be possible to organize life in any other way. Yet one of the miracles of human existence is the tremendous variety that occurs in such basic matters as this. For instance, the Hopi are separated from us by a tremendous cultural gulf. Time, for example, is not duration but many different things for them. It is not fixed or measurable as we think of it, nor is it a quantity. It is what happens when the corn matures or a sheep grows up—a characteristic sequence of events. It is the natural process that takes place while living substance acts out its life drama. Therefore, there is a different time for everything which can be altered by circumstances. One used to see Hopi houses that were in the process of being built for years and years. Apparently the Indians had no idea that a house could or should be built in a given length of time since they could not attribute to it its own inherent time system such as the corn and the sheep had. This way of looking at time cost the government untold thousands of dollars on construction projects because the Hopi could not conceive of there being a fixed time in which a dam or a road was supposed to be built. Attempts to get them to meet a schedule were interpreted as browbeating and only made things worse.

It was mentioned earlier that in contrast to some of the African systems, the components of American time—the minutes, the hours—have to add up. Americans start with the assumption that they are working with a *synthesized* system. Basically the reason why time has to add up is that we start with the assumption that we are dealing with a system and that there is order in the universe. We feel it is mankind's job to discover the order and to create intellectual models that reflect it. We are driven by our own way of looking at things to synthesize almost everything. Whenever we have to deal with people whose time systems lack this isolate of synthesisity we experience great difficulty. To us it's almost as if they were missing one of their senses and were therefore unaware of part of nature. The synthesisity isolate is basic to most if not all of our appraisal of life around us.

Americans consider *depth* as a necessary component of time; that is, there is a past on which the present rests. Yet we have not elaborated the depth isolate to the extent that this has been done in the Middle East and South Asia. The Arab looks back two to six thousand years for his/her own origins. History is used as the basis for almost any modern action. The chances are that Arabs won't start a talk or a speech or analyze a problem without first developing the historical aspects of their subject. Americans assume that time has depth but they take this for granted.

Most of the formal patterns of time in the United States will seem immediately obvious to the American readers though they may not have taken the trouble to think about them. They would not be formal patterns if they were not so easily recognized. But for the benefit of the foreign reader I will summarize briefly the American formal pattern.

Americans seldom question the fact that time should be planned and future events fitted into a schedule. We think that people should look forward to the future and not dwell too much on the past. Our future is not remote. Results must be obtained in the foreseeable future—one or two years or at the most five or ten. Promises to meet deadlines and appointments are taken very seriously. There are real penalties for being late and for not keeping commitments in time. From this it can be surmised that the American thinks it is natural to quantify time. To fail to do so is unthinkable. The American specifies how much time it requires to do everything. "I'll be there in ten minutes." "It will take six months to finish that job." "I was in the Army for four and a half years."

The Americans, like so many other people, also use time as a link that chains events together. *Post hoc, ergo propter hoc* (after the fact, therefore because of the fact) is still an integral part of the traditional structure of our culture. The occurrence of one event on the heels of another results inevitably in attempts on our part to attribute the second to the first and to find a causal relationship between them. If A is seen in the vicinity of B's murder shortly after the crime has been committed we automatically form a connection between A and B. Conversely, events which are separated by too much time are difficult for us to connect in our minds. This makes it almost impossible for us as a nation to engage in long-range planning.

INFORMAL TIME: SETS, ISOLATES, AND PATTERNS

To complicate matters for the young who are trying to learn the culture and the scientist who is trying to analyze it, the vocabulary of informal time is often identical with that of technical and formal time. Words such as minute, second, year are common to all three. The context usually tells the hearer which level of discourse is being used. There are, of course, words which are typically informal and are recognized as such (a while, later, a long time, etc.). In describing informal time we begin with the sets, because it is the set that is most easily perceived.

When a person says, "It'll take a while," you have to know her/him personally and also a good deal about the total context of the remark before you can say what the term "a while" means. Actually, it is not as vague as it seems at first, and people who have this information can usually tell what is meant. What is more, if a man whose normal "while" is thirty to forty-five minutes returns to his office after an hour, having said he would only be gone for "a while," he will usually apologize or make some remark about having been gone longer than he expected. This is proof that he himself realized that there was a limit to the degree to which you stretch "a while."

The basic vocabulary of informal time is simple. There are only eight or nine different distinctions made by Americans. It is as if we measured informal time with a rubber ruler which could be infinitely expanded or compressed but which would still maintain the integrity of the basic relationships. The shortest time on the informal scale is the "instantaneous event." The following additional distinctions are interposed between the "instantaneous event" and "forever": very short duration, short duration, neutral duration (neither noticeably short nor long), long duration, very long duration, and impossibly long duration. The last is sometimes indistinguishable from "forever."

In general, informal time is quite vague because it is situational in character. The circumstances vary, hence the measured time varies: The "longest time," "forever," and "an eternity" are all words or expressions which are used to describe any time which is experienced as being excessively drawn out. Depending on circumstances, "eternity" may be the time it takes to hit the water when one jumps from a high diving board for the first time, or it may be a month spent overseas away from one's family.

Informally, for important daytime business appointments in the eastern United States between equals, there are eight time sets in regard to punctuality and length of appointments: on time, five, ten, fifteen, twenty, thirty, forty-five minutes, and one hour early or late. Keeping in mind that situations vary, there is a slightly different behavior pattern for each point, and each point on the scale has a different meaning. As for the length of appointments an hour with an important person is different from thirty minutes with that same person. Ponder the significance of the remark, "He spent over an hour closeted with the President." Everyone knows the business must have been important. Or consider, "He could only spare ten minutes, so we didn't get much accomplished." Time then becomes a message as eloquently direct as if words were used. As for punctuality no right-minded American would think of keeping a business associate waiting for an hour; it would be too insulting. No matter what is said in apology, there is little that can remove the impact of an hour's heel-cooling in an outer office.

Even the five-minute period has its significant subdivisions. When equals meet, one will generally be aware of being two minutes early or late but will say nothing, since the time in this case is not significant. At three minutes a person will still not apologize or feel that it is necessary to say anything (three is the first significant number in the one-to-five series); at five minutes there is usually a short apology; and at four minutes before or after the hour the person will mutter something, although he/she will seldom complete the muttered sentence. The importance of making detailed observations on these aspects of informal culture is driven home if one pictures an actual situation. An American ambassador in an unnamed country interpreted incorrectly the significance of time as it was used in visits by local diplomats. An hour's tardiness in their system is equivalent to five minutes by ours, fifty to fifty-five minutes to four minutes, forty-five minutes to three minutes, and so on for daytime official visits. By their standards the local diplomats felt they couldn't arrive exactly on time; this punctuality might be interpreted locally as an act relinquishing their freedom of action to the United States. But they didn't want to be insulting—an hour late would be too late—so they arrived fifty minutes late. As a consequence the ambassador said. "How can you depend on these people when they arrive an hour late for an appointment and then just mutter something? They don't even give you a full sentence of apology!" He couldn't help feeling this way, because in American time fifty to fifty-five minutes late is the insult period, at the extreme end of the duration scale, yet in the country we are speaking of it's just right.

For another way of apportioning informal time consider the eastern Mediterranean Arabs, who make fewer distinctions than we do. Their scale has only three discernible points to our eight. Their sets seem to be: no time at all; now (or present), which is of varying duration; and forever (too long). In the Arab world it is almost impossible to get someone to experience the difference between waiting a long time and a very long time. Eastern Mediterranean Arabs simply do not make this temporal distinction.

Informal time isolates will be more significant to the readers if they will sit back for a minute and think in some detail about times when they were aware that time was either passing very rapidly or else dragging. It may even be helpful if they will note what it was in the situation that made time behave the way it did. If they will go even further and think at length about how they were able to distinguish between a very short time and a long time regardless of the clock time, they will be well on the road to understanding how the American system works. What follows below merely attempts to simply put into words things that people know but have not formulated precisely.

Four isolates enable people to distinguish between the duration sets mentioned above. The most difficult of all to characterize, they are: urgency, monochronism, activity, and variety.

The impression of time as passing rapidly or slowly is related to *urgency*. The more urgent the need, the more time appears to drag. This applies to everything from basic physiological needs to culturally derived needs. A man who has an urgent need to succeed and reach the top will experience the passage of time on the way up with more anguish than will another man who is more relaxed about success. The parent with a sick child desperately in need of medical attention feels time moving very slowly; so does the farmer whose crops are withering for lack of rain. One could list many more examples. However, more to the point is what is not included when we consider urgency as an informal temporal isolate: First, urgency on different levels of analysis is both a set and a pattern. Second, our own variety of urgency distinguishes us from the rest of western European culture. A lack of a sense of urgency has been very apparent to Americans traveling abroad.

Even physiological urgency is handled quite differently by people around the world. In many countries people need less of what Americans would call urgency in order to discharge a tension. In the United States the need must be highly critical before people act.

The distribution of public toilets in America reflects our tendency to deny the existence of urgency even with normal physiological needs. I know of no other place in the world where anyone leaving home or office is put to periodic torture because great pains have been taken to hide the location of rest rooms. Yet Americans are the people who judge the advancement of others by their plumbing. You can almost hear the architect and owner discussing a new store's rest room. Owner: "Say, this is nice! But why did you hide it? You'd need a map to find it." Architect: "I'm glad you like it. We went all out on this washroom, had a lot of trouble getting that tile to match. Did you notice the anti-splash aerated faucets on the wash basins? Yes, it would be a little hard to find, but we figure people wouldn't use it unless they had to, and then they could ask a clerk or something."

Monochronism means doing one thing at a time. American culture is characteristically *monochronic*. As Americans we find it disconcerting to enter an office overseas with an appointment only to discover that other matters require the attention of the person we are to meet. Our ideal is to center the attention first on one thing and then move on to something else.

North Europeans and those of us who share in this culture make a distinction between whether or not a person is engaged in an *activity*. In fact, we distinguish between the "active" and "dormant" phases of everything. I therefore refer to this isolate, in terms of its Latin root, as an *ageric* isolate (from *agere,* to act). Just plain sitting, trying to capture a sense of self, is not considered to be *doing anything.* Hence, such remarks as, "You didn't seem to be doing anything, so I thought I would stop in and talk to you for a while." The exception is, of course, prayer, which has special and easily identified postures associated with it.

In a number of other cultures, including the Navajo, Trukese, eastern Mediterranean Arab cultures, Japanese, and many of those of India, just plain sitting is doing something. The distinction between being active or not is not made. Thus there are ageric cultures and non-ageric ones. A culture is non-ageric if, in the process of handling the matter of "becoming later," it makes no difference whether you do something or not. With us, we have to work to get ahead. We do not get ahead automatically. In the cultures mentioned above, this is not nearly so important.

Variety enables us to distinguish between intervals such

as short duration and long duration, or long duration and very long duration. Variety is a factor in boredom, while the degree of boredom experienced depends on how rapidly time passes.

We look for variety in occupations, careers, and hobbies. Our public "demands" a variety of material objects, food, clothing, and so forth. Consider for a moment the fact that few of us can say what we are going to have for lunch or dinner three days from now, let alone next year. Yet there are millions of people in the world who know exactly what they are going to have, if they are to have anything at all. They will eat the same thing they had today, yesterday, and the day before.

For us it is a matter of importance whether or not there is variety in life. Take the teen-age girl who complains to her mother that there weren't any boys at the dance, meaning that there weren't any new boys. Our demand for variety and for something new would seem to exceed that of almost any other culture in the world today. It is necessary to an economy like ours. Without constant innovation we could never keep our industrial plant expanding.

On the informal level of time the basic distinction is between sameness and variety. With variety, time moves more rapidly. People who are imprisoned away from light where they cannot tell whether it is day or not apparently lose practically all sense of the passage of time. They become disoriented and if kept away long enough they may "lose their minds."

As was the case with activity, we associate variety with external events. Maturing and aging—just getting old— are not considered by us to constitute variety except in someone else, so that we will say, "My, he certainly has aged a lot since I last saw him." To the Pueblo of New Mexico, however, aging is something to be experienced. It means increased stature in the community and a greater part in decision making. Variety, from this point of view, is a natural part of living, and an inherent aspect of the self, providing a basically different view of life from our own.

To summarize this discussion of informal time isolates we can say that Americans determine relative duration by four means: degree of urgency, whether they are trying to do more than one thing at a time, whether they are busy or not, and the degree of variety that enters into the situation. In the informal isolates of a culture, one finds the building blocks of time that go to make up the values and driving forces which characterize a culture.

The informal patterning of time is one of the most consistently overlooked aspects of culture. This is not because people are blind or stupid or pigheaded, although their capacity to hold on to informal patterns in the face of weighty evidence sometimes makes them appear to be so.

It seems that it is impossible to participate in two different patterns at the same time. As I will illustrate below, a person has to stop using one in order to take up another. Furthermore, patterns are anchored, when they are being learned and forever after, in the behavior of groups and institutions. They are the ways of doing things that one learns early in life and for which one is rewarded or punished. Hence, it is no wonder that people hold on to them so tenaciously and look askance at all other patterns.

Informal patterns are seldom, if ever, made explicit. They exist like the air around us. They are either familiar and comfortable, or unfamiliar and wrong. Deviations from the pattern are usually greeted with highly charged emotion because people are not doing things our way. "Our way" is, of course, almost invariably supported or reinforced by a technical rationalization such as the following: "If you are five minutes late for a meeting and have kept ten people waiting, you have therefore wasted almost an hour of their time."

In the United States the nature of the points on a time scale is a matter of patterning, as is the handling of the interval between them. By and large, the space between the points is inviolate. That is, compared to some other systems there is only a limited amount of stretching or distortion of the interval that is permissible. Conditioning for this way of conceiving time begins very early for us. A mother says, "I thought I told you you could play with Susan until five o'clock. What do you mean by staying over there until almost suppertime?" Later in life we hear Father saying to a friend, "I promised to spend an hour with Johnny working on his tree house, and I can't very well get off with much less." And in adult life, "But Mr. Jones, this is the third time Mr. Brown has tried to see you, and you promised to spend at least thirty minutes going over those specifications with him."

Our pattern allows very little switching of the position of "intervals" once they are set in a schedule, nor does it allow for much tampering with either the content or the position of the points on the time scale. An appointment to talk about a contract scheduled to begin at ten o'clock and end at eleven o'clock is not easily moved, nor can you talk about anything but the contract without offending people. Once set, the schedule is almost sacred, so that not only is it wrong, according to the formal dictates of our culture, to be late, but it is a violation of the informal patterns to keep changing schedules or appointments or to deviate from the agenda.

How much this is a factor in other cultures has not been determined precisely. There are cases, however, where the content or "agenda" of a given period of time is handled quite differently. In the Middle East, again, refusal of a party to come to the point and discuss the topic of a meeting often means they cannot agree to your terms but don't want to turn you down, or simply that they cannot discuss the matter under consideration because the time is not yet ripe. They will not, moreover, feel it is improper to meet without ever touching on the topic of the meeting.

Our pattern calls for the fixing of the agenda informally beforehand. We do not, as a whole, feel too comfortable trying to operate in a semi-public situation, hammering out an agenda, the way the Russians do. We prefer to assume that both parties want to talk about the subject, otherwise they wouldn't be there; and that they are sufficiently involved in the topic to make it worth their while. With the Russians there is some indication that, while this is true, negotiation over the separate points of the agenda signals to the other side how the opponent is going to react during the actual conference. Softness on our part in early negotiation, because we do not technically fix the agenda but agree informally about what should be taken up, is often interpreted as weakness. Or it may give the impression that we are going to give in on certain points when we aren't at all.

Earlier it was mentioned that the content and limits of a period of time were sacrosanct. If, however, the topic for discussion is completed satisfactorily, or it is apparent that no progress can be made, then the meeting or visit may be cut short. This often leaves people feeling a little funny. By and large, the overriding pattern with us is that once you have scheduled the time, you have to use it as designated, even when it turns out that this is not necessary or advantageous.

All of which seems very strange to the Arabs. They start at one point and go until they are finished or until something intervenes. Time is what occurs before or after a given point. The thing to remember in contrasting the two systems is that Americans cannot shift the partitions of schedules without violating a norm; Arabs can. With us the compartments are sacred. If we have allocated so much time to a certain activity, we can change it once, or maybe twice, when we are trying to discover the proper amount of time for the activity. We cannot continually move the walls of our time compartments back and forth, even though an activity may actually call for such flexibility. The pattern of the immovable time wall applies in most situations, even long periods of time, such as how long it takes to complete a college career.

It is not necessary to leave the country to encounter significantly different time patterns. There are differences between families and differences between men and women; occupational differences, status differences, and regional differences. In addition there are two basic American patterns that often conflict. I have termed these the "diffused point pattern" and the "displaced point pattern." The difference between them has to do with whether the leeway is on one side of the point or is diffused around it.

Contrasting the behavior of two groups of people participating in the two patterns, one observes the following: Taking 8:30 A.M. as the point, participants in the "displaced point" pattern will arrive ahead of time anywhere from 8 A.M. to 8:27 A.M. (cutting it fine), with the majority arriving around 8:25 A.M. Diffused point people will arrive anywhere from 8:25 A.M. to 8:45 A.M. As can be seen, there is practically no overlap between these two groups.

The reader can recall her or his own behavior during evening engagements. A person asked to spend the evening and arrive about "nineish," wouldn't think of using the daytime "diffused point" pattern. The "displaced point" pattern is mandatory, usually at least ten or fifteen minutes after the hour but not more than thirty-five or forty minutes. If asked for dinner, with cocktails before, the leeway is much less. It is permissible to arrive for a seven o'clock engagement at 7:05 but not much later than 7:15. The "mutter something" period starts at 7:20 and by 7:30, people are looking around and saying, "I wonder what's happened to the Smiths!" The hostess may have a roast in the oven. In New York City there is a big difference between a "5 to 8" cocktail party, when people arrive between 6 and 7:30 to stay for hours, and dinner-party time when ten minutes late is the most allowed.

In these terms, the actual displacement of the point is a function of three things: (a) the type of social occasion and what is being served; (b) the status of the individual who is being met or visited; (c) the individual's own way of handling time.

When a shift occurs in an office from diffused point to displaced point, people feel strongly about it. The diffused point people never really feel comfortable with the other pattern. Such shifts are often interpreted as robbing professional people of status. That is, they *feel* they have been lowered in the esteem of the boss. This is because of the use of this same pattern when meeting dignitaries and when great social distance exists between individuals. The displaced pointers, on the other hand, regard everyone else as very unbusinesslike, sloppy, and as having poor organizational morale. They feel the lack of control and are distrustful of the academic types who are so cavalier about being "on time." Persistent efforts to restrict scientists to the displaced point pattern by enforcing rigid schedules is one of the many things that helped drive many scientists from government work in the last few years.

Regionally in the United States there are seemingly endless variations in the way time is handled. These variations, however, are comparable to the variations in the details of speech associated with the different parts of the country. Everybody participates in the over-all pattern which makes it possible for us to be mutually understood wherever we go.

In Utah, where the Mormons at first got somewhat technical about time and later developed strong formal systems emphasizing promptness, you find the displaced point pattern with very little leeway. That is, the attempt is made to arrive "on time," which means a little before the hour and no more than one minute late. Since, according to their system, it's worse to be late than early, they arrive on the early side of the point, just as military personnel do. What this communicates to other Americans is that Mormons are more serious about their work than the average American.

The northwest coastal region of the United States does some very strange things with time, when looked at in terms of the rest of the country. They will ask a person for 6 P.M. if they want him/her to arrive by 6:30 P.M., and then hope that he/she gets there. The detail of muttering an apology after four minutes is quite uncommon and is decried by many.

The more traditional part of the South, on the other hand, seems to behave pretty much as predicted; people slow things down by allowing leeway in both patterns. One finds a greater permissible spread, or a wider range of deviation from the point, than in the urban Northeast. The same could be said for the Old West.

10

SPACE SPEAKS

Every living thing has a physical boundary that separates it from its external environment. Beginning with the bacteria and the simple cell and ending with humans, every organism has a detectable limit which marks where it begins and ends. A short distance up the phylogenetic scale, however, another, non-physical boundary appears that exists outside the physical one. This new boundary is harder to delimit than the first but is just as real. We call this the "organisms' territory." The act of laying claim to and defending a territory is termed territoriality. It is territoriality with which this chapter is most concerned. In humans, it becomes highly elaborated, as well as being very greatly differentiated from culture to culture.

Anyone who has had experience with dogs, particularly in a rural setting such as on ranches and farms, is familiar with the way in which the dog handles space. In the first place, the dog knows the limits of his master's "yard" and will defend it against encroachment. There are also certain places where he sleeps: a spot next to the fireplace, a spot in the kitchen, or one in the dining room if he is allowed there. In short, a dog has fixed points to which he returns time after time, depending upon the occasion. One can also observe that dogs create zones around them. Depending upon his relationship to the dog and the zone he is in, a trespasser can evoke different behavior when he or she crosses the invisible lines which are meaningful to the dog.

This is particularly noticeable in females with puppies. A mother who has a new litter in a little-used barn will claim the barn as her territory. When the door opens she may make a slight movement or stirring in one corner. Nothing else may happen as the intruder moves ten or fifteen feet into the barn. Then the dog may raise her head or get up, circle about, and lie down as another invisible boundary is crossed. One can tell about where the line is by withdrawing and watching when her head goes down. As additional lines are crossed, there will be other signals, a thumping of the tail, a low moan or a growl.

One can observe comparable behavior in other vertebrates—fish, birds, and mammals. Birds have well-developed territoriality, areas which they defend as their own and which they return to year after year. To those who have seen a robin come back to the same nest each year this will come as no surprise. Seals, dolphin, and whales are known to use the same breeding grounds. Individual seals have been known to come back to the same rock year after year.

People have developed their territoriality to an almost unbelievable extent. Yet we treat space somewhat as we treat sex. It is there but we don't talk about it. And if we do, we certainly are not expected to get technical or serious about it. The man of the house is always somewhat apologetic about "his chair." How many prople have had the experience of coming into a room, seeing a big comfortable chair and heading for it, only to pull themselves up short, or pause and turn to the man and say, "Oh, was I about to sit in your chair?" The reply, of course, is usually polite. Imagine the effect if the host were to give vent to his true feelings and say, "Hell, yes, you're sitting in my chair, and I don't like anybody sitting in my chair!" For some unknown reason, our culture has tended to play down or cause us to repress and dissociate the feelings we have about space. We relegate it to the informal and are likely to feel guilty whenever we find ourselves getting angry because someone has taken our place.

Territoriality is established so rapidly that even the second session in a series of lectures is sufficient to find a significant proportion of most audiences back in the same seats. What's more, if one has been sitting in a particular seat and someone else occupies it, one can notice a fleeting irritation. There is the remnant of an old urge to throw out the interloper. The interloper knows this too, because he or she will turn around or look up and say, "Have I got your seat?" at which point you lie and say, "Oh no, I was going to move anyway."

Once while talking on this subject to a group of Americans who were going overseas, one very nice, exceedingly mild-mannered woman raised her hand and said, "You mean it's natural for me to feel irritated when another woman takes over my kitchen?" Answer: "Not only is it natural, but most American women have very strong feelings about their kitchens. Even a mother can't come in and wash the dishes in her daughter's kitchen without annoying her. The kitchen is the place where 'who will dominate' is settled. All women know this, and some can even talk about it. Daughters who can't keep control of their kitchen will be forever under the thumb of any woman who can move into this area."

The questioner continued: "You know that makes me

feel so relieved. I have three older sisters and a mother, and every time they come to town they march right into the kitchen and take over. I want to tell them to stay out of my kitchen, that they have their own kitchens and this is my kitchen, but I always thought I was having unkind thoughts about my mother and sisters, thoughts I wasn't supposed to have. This relieves me so much, because now I know I was right."

Father's shop is, of course, another sacred territory and best kept that way. The same applies to his study, if he has one.

As one travels abroad and examines the ways in which space is handled, startling variations are discovered— differences which we react to vigorously. Since none of us is taught to look at space as isolated from other associations, feelings cued by the handling of space are often attributed to something else. In growing up people learn literally thousands of spatial cues, all of which have their own meaning in their own context. These cues *release* responses already established in much the same way as Pavlov's bells started his dogs salivating. Just how accurate a spatial memory is has never been completely tested. There are indications, however, that it is exceedingly persistent.

Literally thousands of experiences teach us unconsciously that space communicates. Yet this fact would probably never have been brought to the level of consciousness if it had not been realized that space is organized differently in each culture. The associations and feelings that are released in a member of one culture almost invariably mean something else in the next. When we say that some foreigners are "pushy," all this means is that their handling of space releases this association in our minds.

What gets overlooked is that the response is there *in toto* and has been there all along. There is no point in well-meaning people feeling guilty because they get angry when a foreigner presents them with a spatial cue that releases anger or aggression. The main thing is to know what is happening and try to find out which cue was responsible. The next step is to discover, if possible, whether the person really intended to release this particular feeling or whether he intended to engender a different reaction.

Uncovering the specific cues in a foreign culture is a painstaking and laborious process. Usually it is easier for newcomers to listen to the observations of old-timers and then test these observations against their own experience. At first they may hear, "You're going to have a hard time getting used to the way these people crowd you. Why, when you are trying to buy a theater ticket, instead of standing in line and waiting their turn they all try to reach in and get their money to the ticket seller at once. It's just terrible the way you have to push and shove just to keep your place. Why, the last time I got to the ticket window of the theater and poked my head up to the opening, there were five arms and hands reaching over my shoulder waving money." Or they may hear the following: "It's as much as your life is worth to ride the streetcars. They're worse than our subways. What's more, these people don't seem to mind it at all." Some of this stems from the fact that, as Americans we have a pattern which discourages touching, except in moments of intimacy. When we ride on a streetcar or crowded elevator we will "hold ourselves in," having been taught from early childhood to avoid bodily contact with strangers. Abroad, it's confusing when conflicting feelings are being released at the same time. Our senses are bombarded by a strange language, different smells, and gestures, as well as a host of signs and symbols.

However, the fact that those who have been in a foreign country for some time talk about these things provides the newcomer with advance warning. Getting over a spatial accent is just as important, sometimes more so, than eliminating a spoken one. Advice to the newcomer might be: Watch where people stand, and don't back up. You will feel funny doing it, but it's amazing how much difference it makes in people's attitudes toward you.

HOW DIFFERENT CULTURES USE SPACE

Several years ago a magazine published a map of the United States as the average New Yorker sees it. The details of New York were quite clear and the suburbs to the north were also accurately shown. Hollywood appeared in some detail while the space in between New York and Hollywood was almost a total blank. Places like Phoenix, Albuquerque, the Grand Canyon, and Taos, New Mexico, were all crowded into a hopeless jumble. It was easy to see that the average New Yorker knew little and cared less for what went on in the rest of the country. To the geographer the map was a distortion of the worst kind. Yet to the student of culture it was surprisingly accurate. It showed the informal images that many people have of the rest of the country.

As a graduate student I lived in New York, and my landlord was a first-generation American of European extraction who had lived in New York all his life. At the end of the academic year as I was leaving, the landlord came down to watch me load my car. When I said goodbye, he remarked, "Well, one of these Sunday afternoons I put my family in the car and we drive out to New Mexico and see you."

The map and the landlord's comment illustrate how Americans treat space as highly personalized. We visualize the relationship between places we know by personal experience. Places which we haven't been to and with which we are not personally identified tend to remain confused.

Traditionally American space begins with "a place." It is one of the oldest sets, comparable to, but not quite the same as, the Spanish *lugar*. The reader will have no difficulty thinking up ways in which place is used: "He found a place in her heart," "She has a place in the mountains," "I am tired of this place," and so on. Those who have children know how difficult it is to get across to them the whole concept of place—like Washington, or Boston, or Philadelphia, and so on. An American child requires between six and seven years before he/she has begun to master the basic concepts of place. Our culture provides for a great variety of places, including different classes of places.

Contrasted with the Middle East, our system is characterized by fine gradations as one moves from one space category to the next. In the world of the Arab there are villages and cities. That is about all. Most non-nomadic Arabs think of themselves as villagers. The actual villages are of varying population, from a few families up to several thousands.

The smallest place category in the United States is not covered by a term like hamlet, village, or town. It is immediately recognizable as a territorial entity, nevertheless, because such places are always named. They are areas with no recognizable center where a number of families live—like Dogpatch of the funny papers.

Our Dogpatches present the basic American pattern in uncomplicated form. They have scattered residences with no concentration of buildings in one spot. Like time, place with us is diffused, so that you never quite know where its center is. Beyond this the naming of place categories begins with the "crossroads store" or "corner" and continues with the "small shopping center," the "county seat," the "small town," "large town," "metropolitan center," "city," and "metropolis." Like much of the rest of our culture, including the social ranking system, there are no clear gradations as one moves from one category to the next. The "points" are of varying sizes, and there are no linguistic cues indicating the size of the place we are talking about. The United States, New Mexico, Albuquerque, Pecos are all said the same way and used the same way in sentences. The child who is learning the language has no way of distinguishing one space category from another by listening to others talk.

The miracle is that children eventually are able to sort out and pin down the different space terms from the meager cues provided by others. Try telling a five-year-old the difference between where you live in the suburbs and the town where your wife goes to shop. It will be a frustrating task, since the child, at that age, only comprehends where she/he lives. A child's room, house, place at the table are the places that are learned early.

The reason most Americans have difficulty in school with geography or geometry stems from the fact that space as an informal cultural system is different from space as it is technically elaborated by classroom geography and mathematics. It must be said in fairness to ourselves that other cultures have similar problems. Only the very perceptive adult realizes that there is anything really difficult for the child to learn about space. In reality, the child has to take what is literally a spatial blur and isolate the significant points that adults talk about. Sometimes adults are unnecessarily impatient with children because they don't catch on. People do not realize that the child has heard older people talking about different places and is trying to figure out, from what he/she hears, the difference between this place and that. In this regard it should be pointed out that the first clues which suggest to children that one thing is different from another come from shifts in tone of voice which direct attention in very subtle but important ways. Speaking a fully developed language as we do, it is hard to remember that there was a time when we could not speak at all and when the whole communicative process was carried on by means of variations in the voice tone. This early language is lost to consciousness and functions out of awareness, so that we tend to forget the very great role it plays in the learning process.

To continue our analysis of the way children learn about space, let us turn to their conception of a road. At first a road is whatever they happen to be driving on. This doesn't mean that they can't tell when you take a wrong turn. They can, and often will even correct a mistake which is made. It only means that they have not yet broken the road down into its components and that they make the distinction between this road and that road in just the same way that they learn to distinguish between the phoneme *d* and the phoneme *b* in initial position in the spoken language.

Using roads for cross-cultural contrast, the reader will recall that Paris, being an old city as well as a French city, has a street-naming system that puzzles most Americans. Street names shift as one progresses. Take Rue St.-Honoré, for example, which becomes Rue du Faubourg St.-Honoré, Avenues des Ternes, and Avenue du Roule. A child growing up in Paris, however, has no more difficulty learning this system than one of our children learning ours. We teach ours to watch the intersections and the directions and that when something happens—that is, when there is a change of course at one of these points— you can expect the name to change. In Paris the child learns that as she/he passes certain landmarks—like buildings that are well known, or statues—the name of the street changes.

It is interesting and informative to watch very young children as they learn their culture. They quickly pick up the fact that we have names for some things and not for others. First, they identify the whole object or the set— a room, for instance; then they begin to fixate on certain other discrete objects like books, ashtrays, letter openers, tables, and pencils. By so doing they accomplish two things. First, they find out how far down the scale they have to go in identifying things. Second, they learn what are the isolates and patterns for handling space and object nomenclature. First children are often better subjects than second children, because, having learned the hard way, the first one will teach the second one without involving the parents.

The child will ask, "What's this?" pointing to a pencil. You reply, "A pencil." The child is not satisfied and says, "No, this," pointing to the shaft of the pencil and making clear that she means the shaft. So you say, "Oh, that's the shaft of the pencil." Then the child moves her finger one quarter inch and says, "What's this?" and you say, "The shaft." This process is repeated and you say, "That's still the shaft; and this is the shaft, and this is the shaft. It's all the shaft of the pencil. This is the shaft, this is the point, and this is the eraser, and this is the little tin thing that holds the eraser on." Then she may point to the eraser, and you discover that she is still trying to find out where the dividing lines are. She manages to worm out the fact that the eraser has a top and sides but no more. She also learns that there is no way to tell the difference between one side and the next and that no labels are pinned on parts of the point, even though distinctions are made between the lead and the rest of the pencil. She may glean from this that materials make a difference some of the time and some of the time they do not. Areas where things begin and end are apt to be important, while the points in between are often ignored.

The significance of all this would undoubtedly have escaped me if it hadn't been for an experience on the atoll of Truk. In a rather detailed series of studies in technology I had progressed to the point of having to obtain the nomenclature of the canoe and the wooden food bowl. At this point it was necessary for me to go through what children go through—that is, point to various parts after I thought I had the pattern and ask if I had the name right. As I soon discovered, their system of carving up microspace was radically different from our own. The Trukese treat open spaces, without dividing lines (as we know them), as completely distinct. Each area has a name. On the other hand, they have not developed a nomenclature for the edges of objects as elaborately as Westerners have done. The reader has only to think of rims of cups and the number of different ways in which these can be referred to. There is the rim itself. It can be square or round or elliptical in cross section; straight, flared, or curved inward; plain or decorated, and wavy or straight. This doesn't mean that the Trukese don't elaborate rims. They do; it just means that we have ways of talking about what we do and not as many ways of talking about what happens to an open area as they do. The Trukese separate parts which we think of as being "built in" to the object.

A certain decoration or carving at either end of a canoe-shaped food bowl is thought of as being separate or distinct from the rim in which it has been carved. It has an essence of its own. Along the keel of the canoe the carving, called the *chunefatch*, has characteristics with which it endows the canoe. The canoe is one thing, the chunefatch something else. Open spaces without obvious markers on the side of the bowl have names. Such distinctions in the dividing up of space make the settling of land claims unbelievably complicated in these islands. Trees, for instance, are considered separate from the soil out of which they grow. One man may own the trees, another the soil below.

Benjamin Whorf, describing how Hopi concepts of space are reflected in the language, mentions the absence of terms for interior three-dimensional spaces, such as words for room, chamber, hall, passage, interior, cell, crypt, cellar, attic, loft, and vault. This does not alter the fact that the Hopi have multi-room dwellings and even use the rooms for special purposes such as storage, grinding corn, and the like.

Whorf also notes the fact that it is impossible for the Hopi to add a possessive pronoun to the word for room and that in the Hopi scheme of things a room in the strict sense of the word is not a noun and does not act like a noun.

Since there is a wealth of data on how strongly the Hopi feel about holding onto things which are theirs, one has to rule out the possessive factor in Whorf's references to their inability to say "my room." It's just that their language is different. One might be led to assume by this that the Hopi would then lack a sense of territoriality. Again, nothing could be farther from the truth. They just use and conceive of space differently. We work from points and along lines. They apparently do not. While seemingly inconsequential, these differences caused innumerable headaches to the white supervisors who used to run the Hopi reservation in the first part of this century.

I will never forget driving over to one of the villages at the end of a mesa and discovering that someone was building a house in the middle of the road. It later developed that the culprit (in my eyes) was a man I had known for some time. I said, "Paul, why are you building your house in the middle of the road? There are lots of good places on either side of the road. This way people have to knock the bottoms out of their cars driving around on the rocks to get to the village." His reply was short and to the point: "I know, but it's my right." He did have a right to a certain area laid down long before there was a road. The fact that the road had been used for many years meant nothing to him. Use and disuse of space in our terms had nothing to do with his ideas of possession.

SPACE AS A FACTOR IN CULTURE CONTACT

Whenever an American moves overseas, he or she suffers from a condition known as "culture shock." Culture shock is simply a removal or distortion of many of the familiar cues one encounters at home and the substitution for them of other cues which are strange. A good deal of what occurs in the organization and use of space provides important leads as to the specific cues responsible for culture shock.

The Latin house is often built around a patio that is next to the sidewalk but hidden from outsiders behind a wall. It is not easy to describe the degree to which small architectural differences such as this affect outsiders. American Point Four technicians living in Latin America used to complain that they felt "left out" of things, that they were "shut off." Others kept wondering what was going on "behind those walls." In the United States, on the other hand, propinquity is the basis of a good many relationships. To us the neighbor is actually quite close. Being a neighbor endows one with certain rights and privileges, also responsibilities. You can borrow things, including food and drink, but you also have to take your neighbor to the hospital in an emergency. In this regard neighbors have almost as much claim on you as a cousin. For these and other reasons Americans try to pick their neighborhood carefully, because they know that they are going to be thrown into intimate contact with people. We do not understand why it is that when we live next to people abroad the sharing of adjacent space does not always conform to our own pattern. In France and England, for instance, the relations between neighbors are apt to be cooler than in the United States. Mere propinquity does not tie people together. In England neighbor children do not play as they do in our neighborhoods. When they do play, arrangements are sometimes made a month in advance as though they were coming from the other side of town!

Another example has to do with the arrangement of offices. In this case one notices great contrast between ourselves and the French. Part of our over-all pattern in the United States is to take a given amount of space and divide it up equally. When a new person is added in an office, almost everyone will move his or her desk so that the newcomer will have a share of the space. This may mean moving from positions that have been occupied for a long time and away from favorite views from the window. The point is that the office force will make its own adjustments voluntarily. In fact, it is a signal that they have acknowledged the presence of the new person when they start rearranging the furniture. Until this has happened, the boss can be sure that the new person has not been integrated into the group.

Given a large enough room, Americans will distribute themselves around the walls, leaving the center open for group activities such as conferences. That is, the center belongs to the group and is often marked off by a table or some object placed there both to use and save the space. Lacking a conference table, members will move their chairs away from their desks to form a "huddle" in the middle. The pattern of moving from one's place to huddle is symbolized in our language by such expressions as, "I had to take a new position on that point," or "The position of the office on this point is . . ."

The French, by contrast, do not make way for each other in the unspoken, taken-for-granted way that we do.

They do not divide up the space with a new colleague. Instead they may grudgingly give him/her a small desk in a dark corner looking toward the wall. This action speaks eloquently to Americans who have found themselves working for the French. We feel that not to "make a place" accents status differences. If the rearrangement which says, "Now we admit you to the group, and you are going to stay," fails to take place, Americans are likely to feel perilously insecure. In French offices the key figure is the person in the middle, who has his fingers on everything so that all runs smoothly. There is a centralized control. The French educational system runs from the middle, so that all students all over France take the same class at the same time.

It has already been mentioned that ordering is an important element in American patterns. As a general rule, whenever services are involved we feel that people should queue up in order of arrival. This reflects the basic equalitarianism of our culture. In cultures where a class system or its remnants exist, such ordinality may not exist. That is, where society assigns rank for certain purposes, or wherever ranking is involved, the handling of space will reflect this.

To us it is regarded as a democratic virtue for people to be served without reference to the rank they hold in their occupational group. The rich and poor alike are accorded equal opportunity to buy and be waited upon in the order of arrival. In a line at the theater Mrs. Gotrocks is no better than anyone else. However, apart from the English, whose queueing patterns we share, many Europeans are likely to look upon standing in line as a violation of their individuality. I am reminded of a Pole who reacted this way. He characterized Americans as sheep, and the mere thought of such passiveness was likely to set him off crashing into a line at whatever point he pleased. Such people can't stand the idea of being held down by group conformity as if they were an automaton. Americans watching the Pole thought he was "pushy." He didn't bother to hide the fact that he thought we were much too subdued. He used to say, "What does it matter if there is a little confusion and some people get served before others?"

FORMAL SPACE PATTERNS

Depending upon the culture in question, the formal patterning of space can take on varying degrees of importance and complexity. In America, for example, no one direction takes precedence over another except in a technical or utilitarian sense. In other cultures one quickly discovers that some directions are sacred or preferred. Navajo doors must face east, the mosques of the Moslems must be oriented toward Mecca, the sacred rivers of India flow south. Americans pay attention to direction in a technical sense, but formally and informally they have no preference. Since our space is largely laid out by technical people, houses, towns, and main arteries are usually oriented according to one of the points of the compass. The same applies to roads and main highways when the topography allows, as it does in the flat expanses of Indiana and Kansas. This technical patterning allows us to locate places by co-ordinates (a point on the line). "They live at 1321 K Street, N.W." tells us that they live in the northwest part of town in the thirteenth block west of the line dividing the town into east-west halves and eleven blocks north of the line dividing the town into north-south halves, on the left side of the street, about one quarter of the way up the block.

In the country we will say, "Go out of town ten miles west on Highway 66 until you get to the first paved road turning north. Turn right on that road and go seven miles. It's the second farm on your left. You can't miss it."

Our concept of space makes use of the edges of things. If there aren't any edges, we make them by creating artificial lines (five miles west and two miles north). Space is treated in terms of a co-ordinate system. In contrast, the Japanese and many other people work within areas. They name "spaces" and distinguish between one space and the next or parts of a space. To us a space is empty— one gets into it by interesecting it with lines.

A technical pattern which may have grown out of an informal base is that of positional value or ranking. We have canonized the idea of the positional value in almost every aspect of our lives, so much so that even children four years old are fully aware of its implications and are apt to fight with each other as to who will be first.

In addition to positional value, the American pattern emphasizes equality and standardization of the segments which are used for measuring space or into which space is divided, be it a ruler or a suburban subdivision. We like our components to be standard and equal. American city blocks tend to have uniform dimensions whereas towns in many other parts of the world are laid out with unequal blocks. This suggests that it was no accident that mass production, made possible by the standarization of parts, had its origins in the United States. There are those who would argue that there are compelling technological reasons for both mass production and parts standardiza- tion. However, an examination of actual practice indi- cates that Europeans have produced automobiles in the past—and very good ones too—in which the cylinders were all of different sizes. The difference in dimensions was not great, of course, a matter of a very few thou- sandths of an inch. This, however, was enough to cause the car to make noise and use too much oil if it was repaired by an American mechanic unfamiliar with the European patterns that lack the uniformity isolate.

Japan, too, has a passion for uniformity, though it is

somewhat different from ours. All mats (*tatami*) on the floors of Japanese houses and all windows, doors and panels are usually of identical dimensions in a given district. In newspaper advertisements of houses for sale or rent the dimensions are usually given in terms of the number of mats of a specific area. Despite this example of uniformity, the Japanese differ from us in a way which can have considerable economic results. In one case, for example, they manufactured a very large order of electronics parts according to rigid specifications which they were quite able to meet. When the product arrived in the United States, it was discovered that there were differences between various batches of these parts. The customer subsequently discovered that while the whole internal process of manufacture had been controlled, the Japanese had failed to standardize their gauges! It is no accident that in the United States there is a Bureau of Standards. Much of the success of this country's technical skill and productivity, which we are trying to pass on to other nations, rests on these and similar unstated patterns.

HOW SPACE COMMUNICATES

Spatial changes give a tone to a communication, accent it, and at times even override the spoken word. The flow and shift of distance between people as they interact with each other is part and parcel of the communication process. The normal conversation distance between strangers illustrates how important are the dynamics of space interaction. If a person gets too close, the reaction is instantaneous and automatic—the other person backs up. And if they get too close again, back we go again. I have observed an American backing up the entire length of a long corridor while a foreigner whom he considers pushy tries to catch up with him. This scene has been enacted endlessly—one person trying to increase the distance in order to be at ease, while the other tries to decrease it for the same reason, neither one being aware of what was going on. We have here an example of the tremendous depth to which culture can condition behavior.

One thing that does confuse us and gets in the way of understanding cultural differences is that there are times in our own culture when people are either distant or pushy in their use of space. We, therefore, simply associate the foreigner with the familiar; namely those people who have acted in such a way that our attention was drawn to their actions. The error is in jumping to the conclusion that the foreigner feels the same way the American does even though his/her overt acts are identical.

This was all suddenly brought into focus one time when I had the good fortune to be visited by a very distinguished and learned man who had been for many years a top-ranking diplomat representing a foreign country. After meeting him a number of times, I had become impressed with his extraordinary sensitivity to the small details of behavior that are so significant in the interaction process. Dr. X. was interested in some of the work several of us were doing at the time and asked permission to attend one of my lectures. He came to the front of the class at the end of the lecture to talk over a number of points made in the preceding hour. While talking he became quite involved in the implications of the lecture as well as what he was saying. We started out facing each other and as he talked I became dimly aware that he was standing a little too close and that I was beginning to back up. Fortunately I was able to suppress my first impulse and remain stationary because there was nothing to communicate aggression is his behavior except the conversational distance. His voice was eager, his manner

intent, the set of his body communicated only interest
and eagerness to talk. It also came to me in a flash that
someone who had been so successful in the old school of
diplomacy could not possibly let himself communicate
something offensive to the other person except outside
of his highly trained awareness.

By experimenting I was able to observe that as I moved
away slightly, there was an associated shift in the pattern
of interaction. He had more trouble expressing himself.
If I shifted to where I felt comfortable (about twenty-one
inches), he looked somewhat puzzled and hurt, almost
as though he were saying: "Why is he acting that way?
Here I am doing everything I can to talk to him in a
friendly manner and he suddenly withdraws. Have I done
anything wrong? Said something that I shouldn't?" Having ascertained that distance had a direct effect on his
conversation, I stood my ground, letting him set the
distance.

Not only is a vocal message qualified by the handling
of distance, but the substance of a conversation can often
demand special handling of space. There are certain
things which are difficult to talk about unless one is
within the proper conversational zone.

Not long ago I received a present of some seeds and
chemicals along with the information that if I planted the
seeds the chemicals would make them grow. Knowing
little about hydroponics except that the plants should be
suspended above the fluid in which chemicals are dis-
solved, I set out to find a suitable flowerpot. At every
flower shop I was met with incredulity and forced to go
through a routine involving a detailed explanation of just
what it was I wanted and how hydroponics worked.

My ignorance of both hydroponics and florist shops
made me feel somewhat ill at ease, so that I did not
communicate in the manner that I use when I am speaking
on a familiar subject in a familiar setting. The role that

distance plays in a communication situation was brought home to me when I entered a shop in which the floor was filled with benches spaced at about twenty-inch intervals. On the other side of the benches was the female proprietor of the shop. As I entered, she craned her neck as though to reach over the benches, raised her voice slightly to bring it up to the proper level, and said, "What was it you wanted?" I tried once. "What I'm looking for is a *hydroponic* flowerpot." "What kind of flowerpot?" still with the neck craned. At this point I found myself climbing over benches in an effort to close up the space. It was simply impossible for me to talk about such a subject in a setting of this sort at a distance of fifteen feet. It wasn't until I got to within three feet that I was able to speak with some degree of comfort.

Another example is one that will be familiar to millions of civilians who served in the Army during World War II. The Army, in its need to get technical about matters that are usually handled informally, made a mistake in the regulations on distance required for reporting to a superior officer. Everyone knows that the relationship between officers and enlisted personnel has certain elements which require distance and impersonality. This applied to officers of different ranks when they were in command relationship to each other. Instructions for reporting to a superior officer were that the junior officer was to proceed up to a point three paces in front of the officer's desk, stop, salute, and state his/her rank, name, and business: "Lieutenant X, reporting as ordered, sir." Now, what cultural norms does this procedure violate, and what does it communicate? It violates the conventions for the use of space. The distance is too great, by at least two feet, and does not fit the situation. The normal speaking distance for business matters, where impersonality is involved at the beginning of the conversation, is five and a half to eight feet. The distance required by the army regulations borders on the edge of what we would call "far." It evokes an automatic response to shout. This detracts from the respect which is supposed to be shown to the superior officer. There are, of course, many subjects which it is almost impossible to talk about at this distance, and individual army officers recognize this by putting soldiers and junior officers at ease, asking them to sit down or permitting them to come closer. However, the first impression was that the Army was doing things the hard way.

For Americans the following shifts in the voice are associated with specific ranges of distances:

1. *Very close* (3 in. to 6 in.)   Soft whisper; top secret

2. *Close* (8 in. to 12 in.)   Audible whisper; very confidential

3. *Near* (12 in. to 20 in.)   Indoors, soft voice; outdoors, full voice; confidential

4. *Neutral* (20 in. to 36 in.)   Soft voice, low volume; personal subject matter

5. *Neutral* (4½ ft. to 5 ft.)   Full voice; information of non-personal matter

6. *Public Distance* (5½ ft. to 8 ft.)   Full voice with slight overloudness; public information for others to hear

7. *Across the room* (8 ft. to 20 ft.)   Loud voice; talking to a group

8. *Stretching the limits of distance*   20 ft. to 24 ft. indoors; up to 100 ft. outdoors; hailing distance, departures

In Latin America the interaction distance is much less than it is in the United States. Indeed, people cannot talk comfortably with one another unless they are very close to the distance that evokes either sexual or hostile feelings in the North American. The result is that when they move close, we withdraw and back away. As a consequence, they think we are distant or cold, withdrawn and unfriendly. We, on the other hand, are constantly accusing them of breathing down our necks, crowding us, and spraying our faces.

Americans who have spent some time in Latin America without learning these space considerations make other adaptations, like barricading themselves behind their desks, using chairs and typewriter tables to keep the Latin American at what is to us a comfortable distance. The result is that the Latin American may even climb over the obstacles until he or she has achieved a distance at which he or she can comfortably talk.

11

LOOSENING
THE GRIP

The first profound scientific understanding of the nature of culture dates back almost a hundred years. Yet to this day the concept of culture is resisted or ignored by a world which has accepted many more abstract and complex notions. Why? Oddly enough it is not the differences between cultures that breed resistance. These are usually acceptable. Rather, years of experience in trying to communicate the basic discoveries about culture have taught me that the resistance one meets has a great deal in common with the resistance to psychoanalysis which was so strong in its early days. Though the concepts of culture (like those of psychoanalysis) are abstract, they turn out, in fact, to be highly relevant to the deepest personal concerns. They touch upon such intimate matters that they are often brushed aside at the very point where people begin to comprehend their implications. Full acceptance of the reality of culture would have revolutionary consequences.

As a means of handling the complex data with which culture confronts us, I have treated culture as communication. This approach has broad implications for future study, but it offers no quick road to complete understanding. The universe does not yield its secrets easily, and culture is no exception. Yet this insistence on culture as communication has its practical aspects. Most people's difficulties with each other can be traced to distortions in communication. Good will, which is so often relied upon to solve problems, is often needlessly dissipated because of the failure to understand what is being communicated.

By broadening our conception of the forces that make up and control our lives, average people can never again be completely caught in the grip of patterned behavior of which they have no awareness. Lionel Trilling once likened culture to a prison. It is in fact a prison unless one knows that there is a key to unlock it. While it is true that culture binds human beings in many unknown ways, the restraint it exercises is the groove of habit and nothing more. Humans did not evolve culture as a means of smothering themselves but as a medium in which to move, live, breathe, and develop their own uniqueness. In order to exploit it they need to know much more about it.

The realization that formal culture can exert a stabilizing influence on our lives should not be mistaken for conservatism. In fact, an appreciation of the nature and purpose of formal culture should eventually prevent our blind acceptance of the teachings of psychologists and educators who, in their zeal to correct past faults in the system, insist that we spoil our children by not setting any limits and being overly permissive. This permissiveness only means that somebody else, perhaps a policeman or a judge, has to define the limits in life beyond which people simply cannot be permitted to go. We must realize that children must learn the limits just as they must learn that there are certain things upon which they can always depend.

A real understanding of what culture is should rekindle our interest in life, an interest which is often sorely lacking. It will help people learn where they are and who they are. It will prevent them from being pushed around by the more voracious, predatory, and opportunistic of their fellow humans who take advantage of the fact that the public is not usually aware of those shared formal norms which give coherence to our society. These social misfits who lack the security of support which formal culture provides want to destroy things and build power around themselves. The case of the late Senator McCarthy was a classic example of this type of opportunism. If the American public had greater realization that formal norms are not individual but shared, they might save themselves from McCarthyism in any of its future manifestations.

Probably the most difficult point to make and make clearly is that not only is culture imposed upon man but it *is* man in a greatly expanded sense. Culture is the link between human beings and the means they have of interacting with others. The meaningful richness of human life is the result of the millions of possible combinations involved in a complex culture.

As I mentioned in the Introduction, the analogy with music is useful in understanding culture. A musical score is comparable to the technical descriptions of culture that the anthropologist is beginning to make. In both cases, the notation system, i.e., the vocabulary, enables people to talk about what they do. Musically, the process of making shorthand notes does not diminish artists in any way. It simply enables them to transmit to others who are not present what they do when they play. In music it enables us to share and preserve the genius that would ordinarily only reach those who were in the physical presence of the artist. Bach, Beethoven, and Brahms would have been lost to us if they had not had at their disposal the means for writing music.

Like the creative composer, some people are more gifted at living than others. They do have an effect on those around them, but the process stops there because there is no way of describing in technical terms just what it is they do, most of which is out of awareness. Some time in the future, a long, long time from now when culture is more completely explored, there will be the equivalent of musical scores that can be learned, each for a different type of man or woman in different types of jobs and relationships, for time, space, work, and play. We see people who are successful and happy today, who have jobs which are rewarding and productive. What are the sets, isolates, and patterns that differentiate their lives from those of the less fortunate? We need to have a means for making life a little less haphazard and more enjoyable. Actually, we as Americans have progressed quite a long way on this road, compared with people of the Arab Middle East and Turkey, for example. Professor Daniel Lerner, a sociologist at M.I.T., discovered when he interviewed villagers in Turkey that the idea of achieving happiness did not mean anything to them. It had never entered their minds that happiness was one of the things they had a right to expect from life and might strive to achieve. This does not mean that these villagers never have happy moments. Quite to the contrary. It just means that their culture does not include this isolate.

All cultures have developed values in regard to what I have called Primary Message Systems. For example, the values in bisexuality center around preferred and not-preferred types of men and women, idealized models for the children of each sex to follow. Most of these models are formal, some are informal. However, what most cultures do not do is provide anything more than labels for the different types of males or females who are the

models for their children. Modern society has complicated matters because of the increased number of alternatives that are provided the young. If one considers the
Comanche of the early western plains, by way of contrast
to present-day Americans, it is possible to get some idea
of how increasingly complex life has become. A young
Comanche boy knew that he had only two alternatives.
He could grow up to be a warrior or a transvestite, the
term used for a man who wears women's clothes and does
women's work. Everyone had a clear idea of what it
meant to be a warrior and the qualities that went with it.
If for some reason or other a boy lacked the bravado and
bravery necessary to be a good warrior and he was afraid
he would fail, his alternative was to put on the dress of a
woman and take up bead work. There were in Comanche
life only two models for adults; warriors and women. Life
in American culture is not that simple. There is not even
a satisfactory inventory of the categories of males and
females for American culture, although some of the types
are reasonably well known because of a persistent interest
in this subject on the part of contemporary novelists. Not
only must we know more about the alternatives that
confront each of us in our daily lives, but we must also
know the overall pattern of life as well.

For the layman and scientist alike I would like to say
that I feel very strongly that we must recognize and
understand the cultural process. We don't need more
missiles and H-bombs nearly so much as we need more
specific knowledge of ourselves as participants in culture.

APPENDIX I

SCHEMA FOR SOCIAL SCIENTISTS

For the social scientist, the basic contribution of this study lies in eight interrelated ideas:

1. Culture is communication and communication is culture.

2. Culture is not one thing, but many. There is no one basic unit or elemental particle, no single isolate for all culture. There are at least ten bases for culture, all deeply rooted in the biological past, that satisfy the rigid criteria imposed by using a linguistic model for culture.

3. The study of institutions and their structure and the study of individuals and their psychological makeup are excluded from the specific study of culture as it is used here, although they are involved in it on a higher organizational level.

4. Humans operate on three different levels: the formal, informal, and technical. Each is present in any situation, but one will dominate at any given instant in time. The shifts from level to level are rapid, and the study of these shifts is the study of the process of change.

5. Culture is concerned more with messages than it is

with networks and control systems. The message has three components: sets, isolates, and patterns. Sets are perceived and constitute the point of entry into any cultural study. They are limited in number only by the patterned combination of isolates that go to make them up. Isolates are abstracted from sets by a process of comparing sets on the level of differential meaning. Controlled experiments are set up and the subject is asked if he/she differentiates between event A and events B, C, D, X, Y, and so on, until all the distinctions he/she makes have been isolated. Isolates are limited in number. Patterns emerge and are understood as a result of the mastery of sets and isolates in a meaningful context. Patterns are also limited in number.

6. There is a principle of indeterminacy in culture. Isolates turn into sets when they are studied in detail and are therefore abstractions. *The more precise the observer is on one level, the less precise he will be on any other.* Only one level can be studied with precision at any one time, and only one level can be described at one time.

7. There is also a principle of relativity in culture, just as there is in physics and mathematics. Experience is something people project on the outside world as they gain it in its culturally determined form. People alter experience by living. *There is no experience independent of culture against which culture can be measured.*

8. Cultural indeterminacy and cultural relativity are not easy concepts to grasp. They mean more than what is good by one set of standards may be bad by some other. They mean that in every instance the formulae must be worked out that will enable scientists to equate event A^2 in culture A^1 with B^2 in culture B^1. A proper cultural analysis has to begin with a microcultural analysis on the isolate level once the sets have been perceived.

A MAP OF
CULTURE

One of the by-products of our studies of culture as communication is a chart that has proved helpful at one phase in our work. A good deal was learned in the course of developing it, and it still represents the only thing of its kind in existence today. I pass it on to others who may be interested.

My colleague, Trager, and I operated on the assumption that culture was bio-basic and had its wellsprings in a number of infra-cultural activities. We were reasonably certain that we had the basic components of culture since all the systems we developed satisfied the necessary criteria. But what did the totality amount to? Given these systems, could you derive culture out of such a base? Remember one of our criteria for cultural systems had been that each system had to be reflected in the rest of culture as well as reflecting all other cultural systems. This led to the creation of a chart that would show in one place the various combinations of the Primary Message Systems with each other. We began by constructing a two-dimensional grid with the PMS on the left and their adjectival counterparts across the top (see chart).

In this way it was possible to see the types of activities resulting from the various combinations of the PMS, with a chart that turned out to be a sort of cultural equivalent of the periodic tables of chemistry. We took two PMS like subsistence and interaction and asked ourselves the following question: "What are the *economic extensions of interaction* and its reciprocal, the *interactional extensions of subsistence?*" We came up with the "exchange" and "the ecological community." *Economic patterns of association* and *organizational patterns of subsistence* gave us "economic roles" and "occupational groupings"; *instructional results of subsistence* and the *economic results of learning* gave us "learning from working" and "rewards for teaching and learning." In some cases we were puzzled at first as to what to indicate under a given heading. The *protective patterns of territoriality* gave us pause for quite a while until it occurred to us that this was, of course, "privacy" on the individual level, while the *territorial patterns of defense* have to do with the organization of territory as a part of a system of defense (natural barriers, like rivers, mountains, canyons, forests, etc.).

It was discovered that in working with the grid the pattern of analysis imposed its own rules. Whatever we decided on in one part had to be consistent with everything else. For example, we thought for a time that the *recreational extensions of interaction* were pleasure, but the over-all pattern of the chart plus certain self-checking features indicated that "participation in the arts and sports" was a better choice.

Notice of the self-checking features mentioned above came about in the following way: By turning to the chart the reader will note that there is a diagonal from the upper left to the lower right formed by the intersection

A MAP OF CULTURE

Primary Message Systems	Interactional 0	Organizational 1	Economic 2	Sexual 3
Interaction 0	Communication Vocal qualifiers Kinesics Language 00	Status and Role 01	Exchange 02	How the sexes interact 03
Association 1	Community 10	Society Class Caste Government 11	Economic roles 12	Sexual roles 1
Subsistence 2	Ecological community 20	Occupational groupings 21	Work Formal work Maintenance Occupations 22	Sexual division of labor 2
Bisexuality 3	Sex community (class, sibs) 30	Marriage groupings 31	Family 32	The Sexes Masc. vs. Fem. Sex (biological Sex (technical) 3
Territoriality 4	Community territory 40	Group territory 41	Economic areas 42	Men's and women's territories 4
Temporality 5	Community cycles 50	Group cycles 51	Economic cycles 52	Men's and women's cyclical activities 5
Learning 6	Community lore—what gets taught and learned 60	Learning groups— educational institutions 61	Reward for teaching and learning 62	What the sexes are taught
Play 7	Community play—the arts and sports 70	Play groups— teams and troupes 71	Professional sports and entertainment 72	Men's and women's play, fun, and games
Defense 8	Community defenses— structured defense systems 80	Defense groups —armies, police, public health, organized religion 81	Economic patterns of defense 82	What the sexes defend (home, honor, etc.)
Exploitation 9	Communication networks 90	Organizational networks (cities, building groups, etc.) 91	Food, resources, and industrial equipment 92	What men and women are concerned with and own

Territorial 4	Temporal 5	Instructional 6	Recreational 7	Protective 8	Exploitational 9
Places of interaction 04	Times of interaction 05	Teaching and learning 06	Participation in the arts and sports (active and passive) 07	Protecting and being protected 08	Use of telephones, signals, writing, etc. 09
Local group roles 14	Age group roles 15	Teachers and learners 16	Entertainers and athletes 17	Protectors (doctors, clergy, soldiers, police, etc.) 18	Use of group property 19
Where the individual eats, cooks, etc. 24	When the individual eats, cooks, etc. 25	Learning from working 26	Pleasure from working 27	Care of health, protection of livelihood 28	Use of foods, resources, and equipment 29
Areas assigned to individuals by virtue of sex 34	Periods assigned to individuals by virtue of sex 35	Teaching and learning sex roles 36	Participation in recreation by sex 37	Protection of sex and fertility 38	Use of sex differentiating decoration and adornment 39
Space Formal space Informal space Boundaries 44	Scheduling of space 45	Teaching and learning individual space assignments 46	Fun, playing games, etc., in terms of space 47	Privacy 48	Use of fences and markers 49
Territorially determined cycles 54	Time Sequences Cycles Calendar 55	When the individual learns 56	When the individual plays 57	Rest, vacations, holidays 58	Use of time-telling devices, etc. 59
Places for learning 64	Scheduling of learning (group) 65	Enculturation Rearing Informal learning Education 66	Making learning fun 67	Learning self-defense and to stay healthy 68	Use of training aids 69
Recreational areas 74	Play seasons 75	Instructional play 76	Recreation Fun Playing Games 77	Exercise 78	Use of recreational materials (playthings) 79
What places are defended 84	The When of defense 85	Scientific, religious, and military training 86	Mass exercises and military games 87	Protection Formal defenses Informal defenses Technical defenses 88	Use of materials for protection 89
Property— what is enclosed, counted, and measured 94	What periods are measured and recorded 95	School buildings, training aids, etc. 96	Amusement and sporting goods and their industries 97	Fortifications, armaments, medical equipment, safety devices 98	Material, Systems, Contact with environment Motor habits Technology 99

of each PMS with its adjectival counterpart. We observed that in filling in the spaces in the grid those activities above the diagonal were concerned with the individual, those below the diagonal with the group counterparts. Thus the *recreational results of association* are "entertainers and athletes," while the *organizational results of play* are "play groups, teams, and troupes."

The chart as it now stands, along with the rules for its use, is actually a kind of mathematics of culture that will be useful to the specialist and will also have certain other applications worthy of mention. It is, of course, limited by the fact that it has only two dimensions. A three-dimensional chart represents the next logical step but would be vastly more complex.

By looking at the chart the reader will observe that it has no content or substance and is restricted entirely to headings. Its present potential is as a classification system and a check list for behavioral scientists, who, when working on large projects, can be sure that no major categories have been overlooked. It is also a special kind of map of the categories of human activities. As a map it can be useful in allocating and keeping track of work responsibility in group projects by assigning a given area to each worker. The mature student may also find it stimulating to experiment with the chart and what can be done with it. There is more than the one axis indicated by the basic systems that intersect. The various areas of the chart are concerned with quite different things; the upper left portion tends toward formal activities, the middle toward the informal, and the whole lower right side toward the technical. While it is quite apparent that each category is discrete, activities which are related occur in adjacent areas. When developed in detail by the breaking down of each category into its formal, informal, and technical aspects, new dimensions are added.

In recent years a constantly recurring problem is the

classification and codification of data which is accumulating too rapidly for most people to handle. The system presented here has 100 major slots, each representing complexes of activities which can be broken down indefinitely. Each number is permanently identified with a major field—0, interaction; 2, subsistence; 6, learning; 8, defense, and so on. Each of the 100 categories can be quickly subdivided by 10 and each of the resulting subcategories by 10 again. Thus 80 is community defenses, 80.2 the economic aspects of community defenses, and 80.5 the temporal aspects. The advantage of such a system over some others is that it has a theoretical base that gives it a consistency and design lacking in the empirical models.

At this point it's important to draw the reader's attention to the fact that the order in which the PMS are given appears to be highly important. Originally this order was chosen because, given these activities, it was closest to the actual phylogenetic order; that is, the activities are learned and integrated in the life history of each organism. The same order can be found in that organism's evolution. Having established this order we also later observed that each system is paired in a functional way with one another; viz., time with space, work with play. The order is also consistent with these paired relationships. An interesting sidelight on order is that most societies rank the systems differently from the order given. The ranking a society assigns to the systems provides a quick way of getting at a cultural profile that can be compared with others. For example, the United States informants questioned on this departed from the basic order as regards materials, recreation, and bisexuality. As could be predicted for Americans, materials were placed near the top, recreation and bisexuality competed for the last place. An Arab informant differed considerably from the Americans. He separated time and space, putting time last; materials were ranked low, while defense systems were ranked with communication at the top.

Laying out a map of culture is a unique way of proceeding. In the past our data has not lent itself to presentations of this sort. The whole theory of culture as presented in this volume differs in many important respects from previous thought. The principal differences are: (a) the use of a linguistic model; (b) the observation of the whole of culture as communication; (c) the concept of the PMS rooted in biology; (d) the formal, informal, and technical types of integrations; (e) the derivations of these integrations: sets, isolates, and patterns.

The writer and his colleagues who worked with him developing this analysis have found it to be one that is rewarding to work with, enlightening, and conducive to further research. It satisfied our demands for specificity, concreteness, and teachability. We have also discovered that, by sticking to one of the PMS at a time when working with an informant, it is possible to keep a firm footing in the known at the same time that one is getting into new and unknown areas. For example, temporal isolates of the informal variety as elicited from an Arab also shed new light on Arab values in a way that would have otherwise been difficult to achieve.

It is hoped that this brief explanation will serve two purposes: to enlighten the non-specialist interested in cross-cultural work as to the nature of culture and to stimulate students to further work. Much progress needs to be made in the definition of cultural isolates as a means of handling values. It would seem that here we have a few leads as to how this might be done.

APPENDIX III

THREE EXAMPLES OF CHANGE

This appendix has been added for the specialist and represents three clinical case studies of change. They illustrate the progression from formal to informal to technical. The introduction of the initial *v* into English from the French in the eleventh century is an example of diffusion from one culture to another. The screw thread example is picked up at the point where different manufacturers are in the process of giving up their own informal thread design and are willing to submit to the standardizing dictates of the technical. The southwest pottery case is the most technical of all and is reproduced here because of the interest of colleagues in new ways of testing historical reconstructions of the past. It concerns the transfer of an entire technological process, so that it is possible to get a step-by-step picture of how the new technology became integrated, how it also at one moment was freed from the bonds of tradition, and how it later became fettered, but within a new frame of reference.

In England prior to the Norman Conquest *v* and *f* were variants of the same sound (what the linguist calls allophones of the same phoneme). *F* tended to be used in initial position in words, whereas *v* was more commonly used in the middle. The French conquerors, on the other hand, used these two as completely separate sounds, just as we do today.

Included in the cultural impedimenta which the French brought to England were various foods. Among these was veal. Englishmen who spoke French had to learn to make the distinction between *v* and *f*, because now, not only did it make a difference to the finicky French, but a new English word had to be differentiated. Undoubtedly, lower-class Englishmen in time went on talking as though there were no difference. Eventually these informal adaptations of the English were technicalized and the *v* as well as the *f* as an initial consonant began appearing in print in English words as well as in anglicized French words. Today the initial *v* is part of our formal system, and it is unthinkable that anyone would ever seriously consider going back to the old form. The fact that we think of it as right and natural marks it as formal.

THE STANDARDIZATION OF THE SCREW THREAD

One would not expect that something as technical and mundane as the screw thread of nuts and bolts would illustrate, by its history, how changes are made at one point in time and deeply resisted at another. The fact that there is a demonstrable need for change does not necessarily mean that change takes place. How change occurs is a function of whether a given cultural item is treated formally, informally, or technically.

The history of the screw thread begins in earnest with the industrial revolution in England and in this country. In the early days of manufacturing, each factory designed its own nuts and bolts. There was no standardization. Obviously this situation could not go on indefinitely. Yet it was quite a revolution when the American inventor and industrialist, William Sellers of the Franklin Institute, standardized the thread designs of the Americans into one thread which was eventually adopted by the Society for Automotive Engineers. While Sellers was working out the fate of the American nuts and bolts, an Englishman by the name of Whitworth was doing a similar job for the British. Both men's technical solutions to the problem of standardization were so close that the end products were almost but not quite identical. This didn't bother anyone very much until World War I, when the United States began producing war goods for the English and vice versa. When one side made a machine gun for the other, it either had to retool all thread-cutting operations or else make a product that was held together with nuts and bolts that wouldn't fit anything else the end user had. The retooling and stockpiling of nuts and bolts that were almost but not quite identical ran into many millions of dollars. Everyone realized that it would make more sense for both nations to decide on a common thread design, but the idea was strongly resisted. Engineers and administrators treated the problem as a technical one. Actually, once the technical solutions of standardization were separately arrived at by Sellers and Whitworth, each nation treated its own thread design as a formal matter. This meant that those who were involved would resist logic and technical arguments with all sorts of rationalizations, none of which had any technical validity.

Two world wars, the lives of an unknown number of troops who died because they couldn't scavenge ordnance parts in the field, and millions of dollars of added expense all failed to bring about a change.

Informally, different individuals tried to work out solutions. But it wasn't until World War II that William L.

Batt, an American engineer and business executive, managed to mobilize enough support to obtain agreement on a thread design that would be used by both nations in the manufacture of equipment that the other was to use. Finally, with the English conceding more than the Americans, compromise was achieved. The screw thread had been born technically, drifted through a long formal phase, and had at last returned to the technical sphere.

In much the same way, American resistance to adoption of the metric system (a Napoleonic innovation) is without logic. There is no reason why we should hold out, except that weights and measures are to most people formal systems. As Americans we respond viscerally to the idea that we should give up the pound and take the kilo in its place, in spite of the fact that in science and engineering the metric system is gradually taking over.

AN EARLY CASE OF TECHNICAL ASSISTANCE

The next example comes from southwestern archaeology and is concerned with the transfer of pottery making from one group to another approximately fifteen hundred years ago. Pottery is a good topic for examination of change, because pottery fragments are virtually indestructible. Besides, clay has such qualities that it is almost impossible to manufacture pottery without leaving a good deal of evidence as to the method of manufacture. In addition, pottery provides a long, uninterrupted record of any culture.

The example here begins at a time when one of the principal prehistoric cultures of the Southwest had been making pottery for several hundred years. These people are known in the literature as the Mogollon. The name is from the area where their remains were first discovered. The northern neighbors of the Mogollon, ancestors of the present day Pueblo Indians, were known as the Anasazi, a Navajo term for "the old people."

Sometime near the beginning of the Christian Era, the Mogollon learned to make pottery, probably from people to the south of them. Later on the Anasazi borrowed pottery making from the Mogollon. The nature of the culture contact between Mogollon and Anasazi as recorded in the pottery made at the time tells something of the tradition of these two peoples and also provides some psychological insights into their attitudes toward change.

Besides making a pot on a wheel, it can be built up with a coil of clay or patched together or beaten out of a ball. The Mogollon used a very thin coil approximately ¼ to ½ inch in diameter, starting the pot either in the base of another pot (or basket) or by spiraling the coil into a plaque and then working the edges upward into a bowl or a pitcher. Each coil was attached to the one below it by pinching the two together at very close intervals. Before the clay had dried, the pinch marks left as a result of the process of manufacture were partially but not completely obscured by being polished with a smooth pebble. The polished-over corrugations left a dimpled surface characteristic of Mogollon pottery. The pot was then fired in an oxidizing atmosphere, which turned any iron in the clay a bright red. The firing method insured that the pottery would be red in the majority of cases, because the clays of the southwestern part of the United States almost always have iron in them. These processes had been established and were pretty much unchanged for three or four hundred years by the time of the initial Anasazi contact at about A.D. 500–600.

It is possible to reconstruct a good deal about the process that took place when the Anasazi borrowed pottery techniques from the Mogollon. The Anasazi apparently observed pottery making in the process but were not technically instructed, possibly because of a language barrier. It may also have been that the men saw Mogollon women making pots and reported back to their wives and sisters. The reason we know there couldn't have been instruction is because the Anasazi pottery, instead of being red, *turned out* gray, showing that it was fired in a reducing atmosphere without oxygen. We know the Anasazi looked on this as an error in their technique, because they went to the trouble of finding red clay which they ground to a fine powder and used to paint the entire surface of the gray pots. Their image of a proper pot was that it should be red. Even after hundreds of years of weathering, minute traces of this powdered clay can be seen clinging to the sides of small pits in the surface of these early pots. The red unfired clay could not be polished because it was put on an already fired surface. The Mogollon pots all show some polishing.

By A.D. 800–900 the contact between the two peoples apparently was a little closer and some actual instruction took place, at least the Anasazi became more technical in their imitation of the Mogollon techniques. They learned to fire in an oxidizing atmosphere on a wide scale which also enabled them to polish red pots before they were fired. Interestingly enough, having learned how to fire a red pot, they didn't give up their original reduced-firing technique but maintained the two ways of firing side by side for several hundred years thereafter. At the same time, they learned to make the obscured neck-coil pottery so characteristic of their southern neighbors. In order to make this type of pottery, the indented coil has to be left unobscured and smoothed over in a particular way. Unlike the Mogollon, the Anasazi did not have a tradition for smoothing over coils and indentations, and they saw the possibilities in retaining the earlier steps in the process. To them the pinch marks had decorative value. At first they may have seen no reason to go through the additional steps of smoothing out the pinch marks and following this up with polishing, when the pot was to be used as a cooking pot. Some of the early examples of this ware are sufficiently sloppy to give one this impression. It did not take them long, however, to develop the corrugating to an art in itself, and they even went so far as to vary the pinch marks so as to produce a design similar to those seen on baskets. This is one of the many cases whereby a process is freed from tradition (the formal) as it moves across a cultural boundary and becomes a technical matter.

The archaeologist can see tradition (the formal) very clearly at work in both the Mogollon and the Anasazi and can also see in the one instance how an informal adaptation—the use of the red slip painted on after the pot was fired—continued to be used even after the Anasazi knew how to produce permanent red by firing. The development of corrugating itself was an informal adaptation which was later technicalized and finally became a traditional form of southwestern pottery. The same applies to the two firing techniques, one arrived at informally but later technicalized and finally worked into a new formal system that persisted for several hundred years.

One of the most important aspects of a study of change of this sort is that it can be used to test theories concerning the cultural history of the Southwest. For many years there was a big difference of opinion as to whether the Mogollon constituted a branch of the Anasazi or was actually a separate culture. On the one hand, it seemed obvious that each culture had clusters of traits common to both. On the other hand, each had distinctive ways of making pots, houses, and stone tools. If it had been possible to see the actual transfer of pottery making in dynamic terms as functions of a process of change, there could not have been much doubt about the fact that the two were in reality very different even though one borrowed from the other. The Mogollon had different *traditions* and were also only sporadically in contact with the Anasazi. In this light, it would be hard to argue commoness of culture.

APPENDIX IV

SELECTED BIBLIOGRAPHY

Bello, Francis "The Information Theory," *Fortune,* December 1953

Benedict, Ruth *The Chrysanthemum and the Sword.* Boston: Houghton Mifflin, 1946

——— *Patterns of Culture.* Boston: Houghton Mifflin Company, 1934/1946

Dobzhansky, Theodosius "The Genetic Basis of Evolution," *Scientific American,* January 1950

Du Bois, Cora *The People of Alor.* Minneapolis: University of Minnesota Press, 1944

Fortes, Meyer "Time and Social Structure, An Ashanti Case Study," *Social Structure:* Studies Presented to A. R. Radcliffe-Brown. Oxford, 1949

Fortune "Those Incompatible Screw Threads," *Fortune,* December 1948

Freud, Sigmund *New Introductory Lectures on Psychoanalysis.* New York: Norton, 1923

Gillin, John *The Ways of Men.* New York: Appleton-Century-Crofts, 1948

Junod, Henri Alexandre *The Life of A South African Tribe.* London: D. Nutt, 1912–13

Kardner, Abraham *The Psychological Frontiers of Society.* New York: Columbia University Press, 1945

Kluckhohn, Clyde *Mirror For Man.* New York: McGraw-Hill, 1949

Kroeber, A. L., and Kluckhohn, Clyde *Culture: A Critical Review of Concepts and Definitions.* Cambridge: Papers of the Peabody Museum, Vol. XLVII, No. 1, 1952

Leighton, Alexander H.   *The Governing of Men.* Princeton: Princeton University Press, 1945

Linton, Ralph   *The Cultural Background of Personality.* New York: Appleton-Century-Crofts, 1945

————— *The Study of Man.* New York: Appleton-Century, 1936

Lorenz, Konrad Z.   *Man Meets Dog.* Cambridge: Houghton Mifflin, 1955

MacLean, Paul D.   "Man And His Animal Brains." *Modern Medicine,* Vol. 95, 1965, p. 106

Malinowski, Bronislaw   *The Sexual Life of the Savages.* New York: Halcyon House, 1929

Marquand, J. P.   *The Late George Apley.* Boston: Little, Brown, 1937

Marriott, Alice   *Maria: The Potter of San Ildefonso.* Norman: University of Oklahoma Press, 1948

Mead, Margaret   *New Lives for Old, Cultural Transformation. (Manus 1928–1953.)* New York: William Morrow, 1956

Pierce, John R.   *Electrons, Waves and Messages.* Garden City: Hanover House, 1956

Radcliffe-Brown, A. R.   "On Social Structure." *Journal of the Royal Anthropological Institute of Great Britain and Ireland,* Vol. 70, 1940

Riesman, David—in collaboration with Reuel Denney and Nathan Glazer   *The Lonely Crowd.* New Haven: Yale University Press, 1950

Sapir, Edward   *Selected Writings of Edward Sapir in Language, Culture and Personality.* Berkeley: University of California Press, 1949

Shannon, Claude   *A Mathematical Theory of Communication.* Urbana: University of Illinois, 1949

Sullivan, Harry Stack   *Conceptions of Modern Psychiatry,* 2nd edition. Washington: The William Alanson White Psychiatric Foundation, 1947

Tannous, Afif   "Extension Work Among the Arab Fellahin," *Applied Anthropology,* June 19

Trager, George L.   "Language," *Encyclopaedia Britannica,* Vol. 13, 1956, p. 696

————— "Linguistics," *Encyclopaedia Britannica,* Vol. 14, 1956, p. 162

Trager, George L., and Smith, Henry Lee, Jr.   *An Outline of English Structure.* Norman: Battenburg Press, 1951

Trilling, Lionel   *The Opposing Self.* New York: The Viking Press, 1955

Tylor, E. B.   *Primitive Culture,* 7th edition. New York: Brentano, 1924

Useem, John   "Americans as Governors of Natives in the Pacific," *Journal of Social Issues,* August 1946

Whorf, Benjamin Lee   *Language, Thought, and Reality.* New York: The Technology Press and John Wiley & Sons, 1956

————— "Linguistic Factors in the Terminology of Hopi Architecture," *International Journal of American Linguistics,* Vol. 19, No. 2, April 1953

————— "Science and Linguistics," *The Technology Review,* Vol. XLII, No. 6, April 1940

INDEX

ABOUT THE AUTHOR

Anthropologist Edward T. Hall received his Ph.D. from Columbia University in 1942 and has done fieldwork with the Navajo, Hopi, Spanish-American, and the Trukese. During the crucial years of the foreign aid program in the 1950s he was Director of the State Department's Point IV Training Program. From 1959 to 1963 he directed a communications research project at the Washington School of Psychiatry. He has taught at the University of Denver, Bennington College, the Harvard Business School, the Illinois Institute of Technology, and Northwestern University. Dr. Hall is a Fellow of the American Anthropological Association and the Society for Applied Anthropology, and a former member of the Building Research Advisory Board of the National Academy of Sciences.

Best known for his work in intercultural communication, he is a consultant to business and government agencies. Part of the year he lives in Santa Fe, New Mexico, where he writes and does research.

ANTHROPOLOGY

In the everyday but unspoken give-and-take of human relationships, the "silent language" plays a vitally important role. Here, a leading American anthropologist has analyzed the many ways in which people "talk" to one another without the use of words.

The pecking order in a chicken yard, the fierce competition in a school playground, every unwitting gesture and action—this is the vocabulary of the "silent language." According to Dr. Hall, the concepts of *space* and *time* are tools with which all human beings may transmit messages. *Space*, for example, is the outgrowth of an animal's instinctive defense of his lair and is reflected in human society by the office worker's jealous defense of his desk, or the guarded, walled patio of a Latin-American home. Similarly, the concept of *time*, varying from Western precision to Eastern vagueness, is revealed by the businessman who pointedly keeps a client waiting, or the South Pacific islander who murders his neighbor for an injustice suffered twenty years ago.

Cover illustration by Malcolm Tarlofsky
Cover design by Carol Carson

US $11.95 / $16.95 CAN

ISBN 0-385-05549-8

51195

9 780385 055499